TRADING IN SILVER

Also by Paul Sarnoff:

TRADING IN FINANCIAL FUTURES

TRADING IN GOLD

For my beloved grandson, Matthew Jacob

TRADING IN SILVER

*How to make high profits in the
world silver market*

—————— · ——————

PAUL SARNOFF

PROBUS PUBLISHING COMPANY
Chicago, Illinois

© Paul Sarnoff˜ 1988

ALL RIGHTS RESERVED. No part of this publication may be reproduced, stored in a retrieval system, or transmitted, in any form or by any means, electronic, mechanical, photocopying, recording, or otherwise, without the prior written permission of the publisher and the copyright holder.

This publication is designed to provide accurate and authoritative information in regard to the subject matter covered. It is sold with the understanding that the publisher is not engaged in rendering legal, accounting or other professional service. If legal advice or other expert assistance is required, the services of a competent professional person should be sought.

FROM A DECLARATION OF PRINCIPLES JOINTLY ADOPTED BY A COMMITTEE OF THE AMERICAN BAR ASSOCIATION AND A COMMITTEE OF PUBLISHERS.

Library of Congress Cataloging in Publication Data Available.

ISBN 1-55738-044-9

Printed in Great Britain

1 2 3 4 5 6 7 8 9 0

CONTENTS

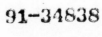

FOREWORD

Investors' reasons for accumulating silver to protect themselves against the ills of inflation, debased currency, etc. are quite understandable. Indeed, silver since Biblical times has been considered 'poor man's gold'. But using silver as a means of trading profits has both its attributes and its dangers.

In this book – for the first time anywhere – the silver physical and paper markets of the world are examined and commented on. Differences in trading approaches and strategies are cited and the author presents lucidly the major fundamental and technical aspects of the silver price.

Whether or not trading in silver will prove successful to readers of this book, who may employ the strategies described here, is, of course, questionable. But each silver speculator and investor participates in the development of a price consensus. Perhaps even more significant (to those who produce and use silver industrially) are the actions of speculators and investors in the various silver markets of the world which provide hedging opportunities, where risk can be readily shifted.

This book provides interested silver speculators, investors and hedgers with the kind of information that could be of assistance in market decisions. It is another educational study by a prolific author whose life has been devoted to changing prices and the value of silver as a truly precious metal.

Dennis E. Wheeler
President and Chief Executive Officer
Coeur d'Alene Mines Corporation

INTRODUCTION

One of the first recorded silver trades appears in Genesis XXIII:16, where Abraham dealt for a burial place for his wife Sarah, paying Ephron the Hittite 'four hundred shekels of silver, current money'. Oddly enough, it turns out that Abraham had previously received from Abimelech, King of Gerar, the sum of 'one thousand pieces of silver' for the King's non-use of Sarah for one night (Genesis XX:16). So it may be held that Abraham profited by 600 pieces of silver – after he deducted the cost of paying for his wife's burial place in the Cave of Machpelah.

In retrospect, it may be also be held that from Biblical times until the late 1960s, when the United States removed silver from circulating coins, silver money was considered 'poor man's gold'. Over the centuries silver, standardised in coin form in relation to a definitive measure of gold, became the prime source of money in circulation. Then when it became more convenient to use paper for currency in circulation, backed by gold and/or silver, this precious metal seemed to become relegated to the small change category for traders and investors.

In the meantime, for the period AD 1500 to 1900 the free market relationship between silver and gold averaged about 15 ounces of silver for one of gold. Perhaps that explains why in the United States for many decades prior to 1968, silver had been fixed by government fiat at a ratio of 16 ounces of silver to one ounce of gold. During the course of history silver prices expressed in paper currency have moved rather violently up and down. On several occasions in mankind's past there have been attempts to corner the available supply of refined silver so that those who contracted to deliver at specified prices found themselves in a bind to obtain bullion. And during these attempts to squeeze the market the price of silver boomed only to crash later when the attempts were aborted.

Silver finally became free from US government constraints in 1968 and then, on 31 December 1974, the government lifted its prohibition against Americans legally owning gold so the relationships between silver and gold in free markets, expressed in dollars and sterling, became rather volatile. The variations in the relationships between one ounce of gold and what it could purchase in the form of silver ounces, and the variations between what one ounce of silver costs in paper currency, including dollars and sterling, for example, have since provided unique opportunities for traders in physical precious metals – and in all silver's leveraged forms, including futures, options and legitimate leverage contracts.

Unlike other books on silver, which delve into great detail about history and oddities involving this remarkable element, this book is designed to cover the ways of profiting from the many methods of trading and speculating, rather than simply accumulating and investing, in silver bullion, coins, collectables and other forms of physical silver. It tries to provide sensible strategies, trading methods and systems that could help alert speculators and traders glean profits in a very volatile medium. Protective measures, always rather rational approaches to profits in silver trading, are also explained. On occasion, both silver producers and silver users may find it useful to trade in the silver futures and options markets as either hedges or something extra added to the price received. In any event, most of the major methods of trading in silver in some form or other are detailed in pragmatically partitioned chapters that cover specialised topics. Chapter 1 covers salient silver forms and facts. Chapter 2 examines the world of solid silver from silver bars to jewellery and their markets. Chapter 3 looks at paper silver and its markets, London, New York and around the globe – both retail and wholesale. Chapter 4 details various silver trading strategies in both the physical and the paper silver markets; whilst Chapter 5 entertains hedging strategies for both silver users and silver producers.

The mechanics of trading physical and paper silver are illustrated clearly in Chapter 6 along with sensible advice on cost-saving in interest, storage and insurance and in transaction fees. Chapter 7 covers the fundamentals of supply and demand while Chapters 8 and 9 look at technical research and trading planning and strategies. The book concludes with a personal glimpse into the future of silver by the author.

1

SILVER FORMS AND FACTS

PHYSICAL AND CHEMICAL PROPERTIES OF SILVER

Silver, in nature, is rarely found in a pure state. Magnificently formed pure silver crystals have been discovered in Michigan; in Norway, embellishing calcite; and in thin sheets extracted by water from host rock. But most of the silver ever mined has emerged from the earth associated with other elements. Readers, who may be interested in delving into silver mining and refining methods are referred to several articles appearing in the *National Geographic Magazine* (September 1933 and September 1981).

Physically, pure silver (99.5 per cent and higher) is highly ductile, malleable, and one of the best conductors of both electricity and heat. The element reflects light more uniformly than any other metal. One grain of silver (0.0020833 of a troy ounce) may be drawn into 400 feet of fine wire, or beaten into silver leaf 150 times thinner than this page. Table 1.1 lists the physical and chemical properties of silver.

Table 1.1 Physical and chemical properties of silver

Chemical symbol	Ag
Atomic number	47
Atomic weight	107,870
Crystal system	face-centred cubic
Melting point (°C)	960.5
Boiling point (°C)	2,212
Electrical resistivity at 20°C, microhm–cm	1.59
Thermal conductivity cal/cm/cm²/sec/°C	0.934 (100°)
Density at 20°C, g per cc	10.49
Coefficient of linear thermal expansion /°C × 10⁻⁵	19.86 (0–100°)
Specific heat at 0°C, cal/g	0.0559
at 100°C, cal/g	0.0568
Periodic classification	IB

USES

Silver is used in a variety of ways in society including photography, x-ray, electronics, space and missile applications – and also the manufacture of jewellery, sterling silverware, silver plate, silver flatware, sculpture, coins, medals and medallions. See Chapter 7 for details of worldwide silver consumption.

SILVER BARS

The basic trading unit of silver is the silver bar. If an investor accumulates bars of silver with a readily recognisable logo or hallmark of an approved refiner, then disposal of the items when required is simpler than for the possessor of silver of uncertain purity. And the investor who accumulates silver jewellery, cutlery, objets d'art, etc. must realise that when these objects eventually are resold to a refiner the craftsmanship value of the silver usually disappears. Not only that, but refining costs will be taken into account when setting the price.

In this connection, therefore, it is suggested that if investors decide to accumulate silver for the express purpose of later resale, they should avoid acquiring any physical silver except standard bars from an approved source. As can be seen in Table 1.2 the investor in physical silver will achieve a better recovery in terms of a percentage of the going silver price with standard bars than with any other silver form.

Table 1.2 Percentage of silver price retrieved on resale of physical silver

Silver form	Percentage of silver price retrieved
Standard bars (1000 oz.)	98%
Small bars (100 oz. and less)	80–90%
Silver bullion coins	80%
Silver flatware	50%
Silver jewellery	20–25%

Source: The Metals Consultancy

To further explain the above table, standard silver bars are in so-called 1,000 ounce denominations of 99.9 per cent silver with the hallmark of a smelter or refiner, acceptable to the London Metal Exchange (hereinafter LME), the New York Commodity Exchange (hereinafter COMEX – see pages 25 and 27 for further details), the Chicago Board of Trade (hereinafter CBOT) or to all three.

A 1,000-ounce silver bar, which looks like a one-pound loaf of bread, is rarely, if ever, exactly 1,000 ounces. The chances are that the vault ticket on the 1,000-ounce silver bar in an exchange-approved warehouse will read something like 1001.5 oz, or 998.5 oz. Some years ago Engelhard (a company prominent in silver alloying and marketing) fashioned 1,000-ounce bars that weighed exactly 1,000 ounces, but they carried a significant fabrication charge. This charge is normally added to any non-standard silver bar weighing less than the 1,000 approximate ounces. As the size of the bar gets smaller, the fabrication charge gets larger. Thus depending on where the bars are bought in the retail market, the charge for fabrication increases as the bar size decreases. For example, 100-ounce silver bars might bear a fabrication charge that varies from 25 cents to 50 cents an ounce added to the price of silver when purchased. Ten-ounce bars might have 75 cents an ounce added. And one-ounce bars generally bear a fabrication charge of about $1.25 above the going spot silver price at time of purchase.

For example, if an investor desired to accumulate silver in 100-ounce bar form, and the going market was $7.50 an ounce for standard bars, the 100-ounce bars (before commissions or other charges) would cost say $8.00 an ounce ($7.50 silver price plus 50 cents an ounce fabrication charge). In an investor accumulated the silver in 10-ounce bar form, the cost would be, when silver went for $7.50 an ounce, probably $8.25 (before commissions). If the accumulator chose to stockpile one-ounce bars then the transaction when silver traded at $7.50 would involve a cost of $8.75 for the silver ounces purchased in one-ounce form. The chances are that when the investor who acquired silver in any of the fabricated forms above went to resell the silver to the original vendor or to any other source, the cost of fabrication would be lost.

In addition to the expense of paying for fabrication in various forms for silver bars, the investor is faced with the questions of either taking delivery of the actual physical bars, or leaving them in a safe depository. Naturally, when small amounts are involved an investor can take delivery and store the silver in a safe deposit box, in a closet, under the bed or wherever. If the silver stockpile, for example, is being gradually accumulated via purchase of small bars and taken home for safekeeping, there is always the danger of robbery. And if the physical silver is in large enough quantities in standard bars to be too huge for safe deposit boxes then it has to be stored at banks that have safekeeping facilities for pallets of the silver 'loaves' which weigh 70 pounds each.

Insurance costs must also be borne in mind. As an example, in 1980 the Bank of Delaware charged 0.0025 per cent per annum of the silver price for storage and insurance by Lloyd's of London against any catastrophe except nuclear war. So when physical silver, in bar or coin form, is purchased and stored there is added expense of storage and insurance if the stockpile exceeds what can be conveniently stowed away in a safe deposit box.

In many states and areas there are taxes upon purchase of silver bullion and coins if delivery is taken. To avoid this investors can arrange for purchase and storage outside their state, or in some cases even avoid the storage charge altogether if they buy 'consigned' or 'pooled' silver (silver which is stored in lump fashion for a number of owners by the bullion source). Details of these operations vary with the retail source and should be checked out before any purchase.

COINS AND MEDALS

In addition to bars there are silver coins. These may be classified as bullion, semi-numismatic, and numismatic coins. Chapter 2 covers numismatics in depth, but at this point it may be noted that no numismatic legal tender gold coin ever carried the resale price that some rare silver coins have achieved. It also naturally follows that silver coins of collector or numismatic quality are subject to the demands of other collectors and necessarily subject to the vagaries of a market where avid collectors may pay big prices for antiques but are greatly saddened when they have to resell suddenly in a dull market.

So that at this point the silver coin market involves mainly bullion coins and semi-numismatic coins.

By definition a bullion coin is a legal tender coin struck by a government in order for the government to earn 'seignorage' (a profit on the fabrication of the coins). The most widely publicised and popular silver coin of this nature is the silver 'walking Liberty' dollar, also known as the 'silver eagle' issued initially in 1986 by the US Mint in order to (a) reduce the amount of silver in the US national stockpile; (b) provide silver in convenient form to American citizens once again; (c) help create demand for silver possibly to help American mining interests; and (d) add to what the Silver Users Association has considered the available silver surplus.

The silver eagle bullion coin, which bears a legal tender value of $1, is distributed to the public by authorised dealers, who buy the coins from the US Mint directly and then retail them to the investing public. The Mint charges $1 fabrication charge above the silver price to the wholesale dealers; and the dealers charge the public whatever the traffic will bear. For example, in 1987, with silver at about $7.50, prices for these coins varied from $9.95 to $25. The best deal was advertised in the *Wall Street Journal* by MONEX (a Newport Beach precious metals firm) of 500-coin lots at $1.35 a coin over the silver price. But while most of the 1986 issue of these bullion coins was marketed at about $9.95,

advertisements were appearing in 1987 for business strike (uncirculated) coins at $18 to $25 because of their rarity (the 1986 minting date).
The 1986 proof coins of this issue, which were sold by the Mint for $24,
were being advertised at $75 by dealers by the end of 1987.

In the United States, Engelhard and Sunshine Mining offer one-
ounce silver medallions which look exactly like coins and are pure
silver. Johnson Matthey offer pure silver one-ounce wafers. These can
be obtained from various agents, including banks and stockbrokers.
Mexico, some years ago, launched a campaign to get something more
than the going silver price by minting coins in varying amounts of silver,
finally settling on the famous *onza*, which contains one ounce of pure
silver. This coin probably bears the lowest fabrication charge of any of
the bullion coins; and is sold broadly across the United States at coin
dealers, some stock brokerage firms and banks.

Having touched upon bullion coins, what are semi-numismatic
coins? Here we have a broad category that includes, for example, silver
coins which were in circulation in America and elsewhere prior to 1965,
when the Government stopped putting silver in dimes and quarters and
reduced the silver in half-dollars. Probably the most publicised semi-
numismatic coins are the Morgan silver dollars, in circulated condition.
Uncirculated and proof Morgan dollars are considered collector-items
and thus numismatic. But the run-of-the-mill silver dollars that have a
face value of $1 each and contain 90 per cent silver, may go anywhere
from $12 to $25. It is possible to buy these coins by mail order, but a wise
investor would probably buy newly minted silver bullion coins from a
reliable source who will buy them back readily and fairly, a source that
will still be in business to buy them back when the coins appreciate in
value. The United States is not the only country to mint silver bullion
coins. Around seventy countries issue bullion coins minted from silver.
See Further reading, Appendix B for details.

SILVERWARE AND JEWELLERY

When silver in January 1980 headed towards $50 an ounce, owners of
silver jewellery, sterling flatware, silver candlesticks, etc., headed with
their heirlooms for the nearest point where they could turn the silver
into money. The result was that a flood of silver scrap hit the market,
helping to send the silver price down from $50 in January to $10.80 in
March. Were those who turned in silver candelabra, tea and coffee pots
fashioned in the nineteenth century aware of the beauty and the worth
of the items they were trading for money? Obviously not, because in the
first place – if they received fair treatment by the recyclers, which is
indeed doubtful – the sellers got only the estimated value of the weight

and the purity in the objects they were selling. Note that in a well-fashioned sterling silver teaspoon (92.5 per cent silver, 7.5 per cent copper) there is about an ounce of silver. To ensure that readers are familiar with, purity and fineness of silver objects, see Table 1.3.

Table 1.3 Purity and fineness of silver objects

Object	Degree of silver fineness or purity %
Silver bars	99.9
Silver bullion coins	99.9
American pre-1965 coins	90.0
Mexican onzas	99.9
Other Mexican silver coins	50–70
Sterling silver	92.5
Silver jewellery (not sterling)	80

Source: The Metals Consultancy

Silver in physical form can be accumulated, like any other precious commodity. But since 1,000 ounces weighs 70 lbs, a sizable amount of silver has to be kept in a safe place, creating costs for storage and insurance. Moreover, in many areas and states, possession of physical silver triggers onerous sales and use taxes. The most economical way to buy silver is to deal with a reliable firm that will store the silver for the investor in a consignment or pooled form so that charges are minimised. If concerned and distrustful of the source from whence silver is purchased and possession is desired, the silver should be purchased with bank delivery and storage. Investors who fear that someday the United States might again confiscate physical silver can store their holdings in England or on the Continent. In fact, at the start of the decade 1980–1990, the Swiss banks in Zurich had to expand their storage facilities to accommodate the silver that was flowing to an area of presumed confidentiality.

Silver in coin form is more expensive to accumulate than in bar form, and silver jewellery should be purchased for the benefit of the beholder since it is a rather costly means of acquiring the metal.

2

TRADING IN SOLID SILVER

Suddenly the silver price – as it has done on numerous other daily occasions in the past – advances by 25 cents an ounce (from $7.50 to $7.75). What is the significance of this to silver investors and silver traders?

To the silver investor, who has accumulated a stockpile of silver bars, coins, or bags of coins, it indicates that the value of the physicals in portfolio has increased. Assuming the physical silver owner holds 10,000 ounces, an improvement of $2,500 is apparent before any liquidation costs (i.e. costs involved in selling the silver).

It is also apparent that if the accumulated physical silver costs an average of $7.50 an ounce, the paper rise in value on the paid-for silver would be a gross of $2,500 on an investment of $75,000. From a percentage appreciation view, the stockpile of silver, therefore, has advanced in a single day some 3.33 per cent. But in order to obtain the benefits of assuming risks in purchase of physical silver, and paying for it in full, the holder of the metal would have to sell off the silver. Of course, if the owner of the physical silver borrowed on it, he or she could obtain the $2,500 market increase; but naturally would owe the loan source the money (thus paying interest on an increase in equity). Moreover, during the time the owner of the silver has held the physicals, the principal (in this case the $75,000 for the 10,000 silver ounces) has lost both the use of, and the theoretical interest income, from the $75,000 required to pay for the 10,000 silver ounces.

For the trader whose primary interest lies in attempting to profit when the price of silver rises, it is necessary to answer the following questions: what are the costs of acquiring the physical form of silver to be traded?; and how liquid are the markets for the various forms?

Purchase of silver bars from a retail bullion source may entail a commission, or if there is no commission, a mark up (hidden or disclosed). Before doing any business with any source, it makes sense to find out first how much above the actual silver price the buyer is being charged (commissions vary from half a per cent to two per cent of the value of the purchased silver, depending on the size of the order). For this purpose the silver price takes many forms. In the United States, the Handy & Harman silver price, which is made public about noon, New York time each day, is considered the wholesale price (the price at which trade interests deal). In the UK and abroad, generally the London silver fixing (one fixing per day briefly after the gold fixing in the morning) is the operating guide. After COMEX silver begins trading, the spot or cash month on that futures exchange generally becomes the spot price – if the spot month is active (see page 36 for an explanation of spot prices). If not, whilst COMEX silver futures are trading, the nearest popular future month, less the differential between the months, becomes the rule. In any event, the buyer of physical silver generally pays the spot price – plus the extras to buy. And when selling, if the sales source is an agent, the proceeds are net after commissions have been deducted. If the source to which the physical silver is sold is acting as a principal then there is probably some discount from the spot price depending, of course, on the size of the order. In recent years fixed commissions have been eliminated both in the US and in the UK so it makes further sense to shop around between sources to predetermine transaction charges before purchase or sale.

As a general rule, if buying silver from a reliable source, such as a commodity exchange member, a member or associate member of the London Gold Market, or a member of any organised stock exchange, it makes the most sense to leave the physical silver purchased at the supply source. In this manner, disposal and payment can occur quickly. But if delivery is taken the seller must ship the sold silver to the agent or principal making the repurchase; and payment is held up until the silver has been authenticated as to both weight and purity. The fabrication charge is included in the buyer's cost and this may or may not be returned when the bars or coins are resold. In some cases only half the fabrication charge is returned upon resale, but in most cases the fabrication charge is lost.

Silver certificates, which are pieces of paper representing ownership of silver in storage, can be offered to potential physical silver buyers. For example, in the autumn of 1987 the Government of Mexico, anxious to have some of its silver sold at retail for the benefit of Mexican citizens and others, issued silver certificates representing ownership of silver left in storage in Mexico. So those who may eventually desire to accept delivery of the actual silver might find the Mexican certificates to be of interest.

Much ado has been made in the past about coin bags – and the trading of them at premiums or discounts to the going silver price. By definition, coin bags are $1,000 face value bags of American dimes, quarters or half-dollars (they also used to include silver dollars, but those have long since been separated from the classification 'coin bags' because even the circulated 'junk' silver dollars bring over $10 each in the retail markets of the United States). At one time the New York Mercantile Exchange (hereinafter NYMEX) traded coin bag futures (ten-bag contracts), but ended activity in this area in about 1977. Since then the bags of $1,000 face value silver coins of 90 per cent purity, and in circulated condition, trade in a rather limited dealer market – with published prices in the *Wall Street Journal* listed under the heading Cash Prices on the commodity page. For example, the entry for 14 October 1987 read:

Coins, whol $1,000 face val . . . . . . (a) 5,800   5,715   4,445

By way of explanation, the wholesale offering (a) price per bag of $1,000 face value, circulated US silver coins (without bags of dollars) on Wednesday, 14 October 1987 seemed to be $5,800 per bag. The price for the same item on 13 October 1987 was a bit less, or $5,715. And the price of 14 October 1986 was only $4,445. The price differences involve the relationship between the going silver price and the worth of the contents of each bag if melted down. In this regard, the $1,000 face value of each bag entailed coins of 90 per cent purity that would yield about 710 ounces of silver. On 14 October 1987 the Handy & Harman silver price was $7.785. This figure multiplied by 710 equals $5,527.35, which would probably be the bid to the published offer of $5,800.

It naturally follows that if an investor desired on 14 October 1987 to buy silver coin bags from a reliable source the offering price would be approximately $5,800. If an owner of silver coin bags wanted to liquidate them on that date he would sell them at about the bid of $5,527. In each case, the buyer and seller might have to pay a buy or a sell commission if dealing through an agent. If dealing with a principal, a firm that buys and sells silver bags on its own account, the differential between the published, asked, price of $5,800 and the calculated bid price of $5,527, which represents the spread might be sufficient. In any case, to calculate the value of the silver inside a coin bag, simply multiply the going silver price by 710. Some sources use 712 but since the coins inside the bag have been worn and circulated, chances are some of the silver has been worn away, so that is why the 710 figure is employed.

Medals made of silver to commemorate historic or military occasions have extrinsic collector value, which is understandably difficult to measure. The markets in silver medals seem to be confined to pawn shops, coin shops, so-called mail-in auctions, such as those conducted in the United States by R. M. Smythe & Co. Thus it naturally follows that the prices depend on the person most anxious to do the business. Medallions of the bullion type, such as those struck by Engelhard, Sunshine Mining, and other 'mints', which are not official government coins, are convenient forms of pure silver in small packages that are retailed at the going silver price, plus a fabrication charge, plus a dealer mark up or an agent commission. Upon resale the medallions are subject to a dealer discount from the silver price or an agent's commission deducted from the gross proceeds.

In rating the preference of trading media in the world of solid silver from the standpoint of best to worst when it comes to monetary recovery on the investments when resold Table 2.1 is germane.

Table 2.1 Ranking of solid silver trading media

Silver medium	Ranking (lowest number is best)
Standard silver bars (1,000 oz.)	1
Silver bars (100 oz.)	2
Silver bars (10 oz.)	3
Silver wafers (1 oz.) and silver medallions which are bullion coin substitutes	4
Silver bullion coins	5
Silver coin bags	6
Silver commemorative coins	7
Silver numismatic coins	8
Silver medallions (other than bullion coin substitutes, including religious medals)	9
Silver medals (military)	10
Silver medals (non-military)	11

Source: The Metals Consultancy

PHYSICAL SILVER MARKETS

In corners on the narrow, winding streets of Stanley Market in Hong Kong, groups of sellers squat over piles of ancient pieces of metal. Among the drab debris at their feet are objects formed of silver, including alleged silver coins. On a hill above Macao, portable stands looking like pushcarts, display souvenirs for tourists which understandably include assortments of silver coins from the exotic Asian past.

Many of these 'silver' coins are relegated to the category 'trade dollars'. That term broadly labels those silver coins circulating in pre-Communist China used as 'poor man's gold'. And the polite vendor of these 'silver' trade dollars readily reveals that these coins were smuggled in by junk captains, who swapped them in Macao and Hong Kong for western goods, including radios. Without casting any aspersions on legitimate people who sell authentic merchandise all over the world, the chances are that if a tourist buys a so-called silver trade dollar from a street vendor or pedlar in either Stanley Market or Macao, and thereupon puts the coin into his pocket to carry around for luck, as so many Orientals do, in time – and after some wear – the true nature of the coin may shine through the outer layer of silver. And the buyer who paid for silver suddenly is faced with a brass coin that has been cleverly silvered.

The moral of this is that potential silver buyers, traders, and speculators should never buy silver from unknown sources – and the sources should be known for reliability. All over the world at some hour of the 24-hour day transactions to buy and sell physical silver in some form or other occur. So the important points any person intending to acquire physical silver should be sure of are: (a) proper weight, form and fineness; (b) the ability of the seller to deliver what is bought; and (c) the ability of the seller to repurchase the silver readily upon resale. Even before making any purchases of physical silver from any reliable source, the buyer should be quite clear as to its form, weight and purity before giving the order to buy it.

It may be that the same gold-dealing brokers, banks and bullion firms also dealing round the clock can accommodate not only commercial enterprises; but also serious speculators and silver traders, in both acquisition and disposal of silver any time of the day or night. For example, any of the five strong-fixing members of the London Gold Market, most of the fifty-odd associate members of that market, and global stock broking firms (with metal departments) can accommodate large customers with bank-to-bank silver deliveries anywhere on earth.

A bullion dealer may be held to be a financial intermediary ready to sell to or buy from any facet of the wholesale silver trade. A bullion broker, unlike the dealer who acts generally as a principal, normally matches buy and sell orders on a back-to-back basis, charging either small commissions or making small mark ups. A bullion banker finances silver transactions for customers, commercial and otherwise. Bullion dealers not only include firms like Mocatta Goldsmid, and its American sister Mocatta Metals; but may also include refiners like Engelhard and Degussa, and Heraeus. Bullion brokers can include firms like King Fook, in Hong Kong; Sumitomo Metals in Japan and worldwide; Shearson and Merrill Lynch; whilst bullion bankers include Republic National of New York; Rhode Island Hospital Trust; Dresdner Bank; and Sumitomo Bank. See the section on silver trading, page 64 to 67 for further information on trading in physical silver.

Users of silver, who vary from Eastman Kodak to Wallace International, maintain inventory levels of silver which may or may not be financed. 'Financed' bullion deals in silver may include the following:

1 *Consignment* (where the silver on premises or at a nearby bank belongs to the bullion source but is available to be drawn down when needed by the user, who is then charged with the cost of the metal at time it is used).

2 *Swaps* (where the owner of 999 silver, who understandably employs alloys in his jewellery or silver plate manufacture, swaps the pure silver for the required alloy).

3 *Silver loans* (where an owner of silver inventory desires to borrow on the metal, but also desires at some future date to get the metal back).

4 *Silver leverage contracts*, also called *Forward purchase and sale contracts* (where the silver user or producer contracts to buy or to sell required bullion to be delivered at a specified future date – in some ways similar to a futures contract).

5 *Silver leasing* (where physical silver is rented for periods and replaced by the lessee).

6 *Physical silver options* (where the bullion intermediary for premiums paid by the user agrees to buy or sell specified amounts of silver at a set price at the end of or during an agreed time). If the silver option is European style it may only be exercised by its holder on the last day; if the option is American style the option may be exercised by the holder at any time up to and including the last day of the option.

Obviously then, bullion-trading intermediaries have to have the following attributes:

1 Solid cash resources in the strong currencies.
2 Innovative ability to tailor physical silver purchases or sales to a customer's needs.
3 A network of hi-tech communication enabling them to deal almost instantly in global silver markets.
4 The ability to purchase silver scrap and concentrate, and refine these into good delivery silver bars.

   The Silver Institute publishes a work called *Silver Refiners of the World and Their Identifying Marks*. It reflects names, addresses, phone numbers along with the identifying hall marks of good silver ingots, popularly called silver bars. These commercial silver ingots are at least 999 fine, which means they contain 99.9 per cent silver. Table 2.2 illustrates some well-known brands in the world of physical silver.

   Readers who are interested in exploring the possibilities of trading solely in the physical silver markets of the world could approach any

Table 2.2 Popular silver refiners and their marks

Country	Company	Hallmark	Ingot mark
Australia	Broken Hill Assoc. Smelters	BHAS	—
Canada	Cominco Ltd	TADANAC	
	INCO	ORC	
	Johnson Matthey	JM	
	Noranda	CCR CANADA	—
West Germany	Degussa AG	DEGUSSA	
	W. C. Heraeus	Heraeus	
Japan	Mitsubishi Metal	—	
	Sumitomo Metal Mining Co.	—	
	Tanaka Kikinzoku Kogyo K.K.	TANAKA	
Mexico	Met-Mex Penoles, SA	PENOLES	
Peru	Empresa Minera del Centro del Peru	C P PERU	
South Africa	Rand Refinery Ltd.	R R LTD	
Switzerland	Swiss Bank Corp.	SWISS BANK CORPORATION	
	Swiss Credit Bank	CREDIT SUISSE	

Trading in solid silver

Table 2.2 Popular silver refiners and their marks *continued*

Country	Company	Hallmark	Ingot mark
USSR	Alaverdi, Transcaucasus, Norilsk, Novosibirsk, RSFSR	C.C.C.P.	
UK	Britannia Refined Metals Ltd.	BL Co	
	Engelhard Industries	ENGELHARD LONDON	
USA	Asarco, Inc.	ASARCO	
	Handy & Harman	HANDY & HARMAN HH	
	Sabin Metal Corp.	SABIN	
	Treasury Department	US ASSAY OFFICE	
Yugoslavia	Rudarsko-Topionicarski Bazen	BOR	BOR

of the firms in the countries listed above for assistance. If these wholesale firms will not conduct business with the applicant, they may refer him or her directly to a client of the involved bullion source who will be pleased to deal with the potential silver trader. A retail source recommended by one of the bullion dealing firms mentioned above will probably be quite reliable because dealing on a wholesale basis in silver, like gold, requires creditworthiness which has been long established with the wholesale source of bullion.

If the aim of the investor is to accumulate a silver stockpile a little at a time, then having an account at a bank that offers silver purchases – without levying any sales and use tax – seems to make the most sense. The Bank of Delaware, in Wilmington, Delaware (where there is no sales tax on silver) offers depositors bullion-purchase facilities and stores the metal for clients. If left in storage at the bank, the customer can resell the silver physicals at any time and receive prompt payment. The Rhode Island Hospital Trust in Providence, Rhode Island, also offers silver accumulation accounts (with no sales tax) so that a potential accumulator can add whenever feasible to a growing treasure. And certain stockbrokerage firms in the United States and elsewhere also offer silver purchase plans (where no sales tax is charged if the purchased silver remains at the broker's depository).

In any event, the potential trader should first find out what the charges are to make trades, what the storage charges and shipping charges entail, and what the payment terms consist of – including when payment has to be made on purchase and when the source makes repayment upon sale.

TRADING IN OLD SILVER

About twenty years ago, English antique silver prices were reported to have 'quadrupled over the past ten years'. Since then, the prices of historically important silver pieces – sometimes massive in size – have climbed to levels affordable mainly by museums. Still, it is broadly believed that interested investors can find small English silver items of superlative craftsmanship, and in fine condition, reasonably enough priced to generate profits if held for some years.

In this regard, the small pieces may range from candle snuffers, varieties of spoons, tankards, articles mounted in silver – and even toys. Obviously any of the above items crafted during the reign of George III would command quite a price during the reign of the present Queen.

In like manner, American antique silver – some dating back to Revolutionary War times – works of art produced, for example, by Paul Revere, may be well above the collector's budget; yet American collectors flock to country auctions and sales, to city auctions and sales rooms, to gift and pawn shops searching for items such as the 1897 patented Saratoga sterling potato chip server, an 1867 ice cream knife, or a 1905 patented horseradish spoon.

In retrospect, the urge to amass and to collect antique or 'old' silver really has to have other primary motivations than the urge to buy something beautiful at a cheap price and later resell it to somebody else at a higher price. Perhaps the real secret for the growth of the penchant to collect old silver lies in an observation by Confucius, who admitted: 'I am not one who was born in the possession of knowledge; I am one who is fond of antiquity and earnest in seeking it there'.

Indeed the search for knowledge may be as compelling as the hunger for gain, when it comes to collecting silver. And while the collector may be able to learn all about the origin of any specific piece, its date, its fabricator (and naturally everything available about the silversmith involved), its historical import or significance, the difficulty lies in determining a fair price for resale and finding a liquid market to effect such sale at a fair price.

Readers who may find interesting silver pieces during their travels from Portobello Road in London to Stanley Market, Hong Kong should ask themselves some questions.

First and foremost, is the silver piece under contemplation primarily desired for appreciation and resale; and secondly would the funds required to purchase the piece be put to better advantage somewhere else in the silver trading area?

Assuming that the piece is actually considered for purchase because the buyer believes it will appreciate enough to warrant the investment, what sort of timetable for resale is anticipated? Generally it takes five to ten years to surpass the spread in old silver. That is, the price between what the antique source will sell the piece for and what he would pay to buy it back. Realistically, the collector intent on buying silver to add to a collection already under way, or to start a collection specifically slanted toward concentration on one area of old silver, would be concentrating on building an inventory rather than disposing of it. For example, assume silver spoons were to be the core of the collection. Should the objects be restricted to mote spoons, demi-tasse sterling spoons, soup spoons or teaspoons? Understandably, if serving spoons were desired and the collector came across some piece of rather unusual design and authenticity that fitted into the collection, his or her hunger for it could cloud the realities, pricewise.

Conversely, the collector might find a specific spoon required to complete a set already in portfolio but is faced with the requirement by the vendor that the collector buy not only the spoon he wants but also the seven others of the same make that are being offered by the seller as a set. In any event, before becoming a collector of old silver with the intent to profit by trading in the pieces subsequently it may make sense to learn as much as possible about the areas the budding trader wishes to specialise in. In this regard, in America as in England there are societies of silver collectors. And in every major city in the US and on the Continent there are museums displaying silver as part of their multifaceted collections. These museums have personnel with special-ised knowledge of old silver; and becoming friendly with these people could be quite beneficial.

TRADING IN COINS

Webster's dictionary defines 'numismatics' as the study or collection of coins, tokens, medals, paper money, and similar objects. For the purposes of this chapter, numismatics applied to coins alone is touched upon. Earlier in this chapter a quote by Confucius was cited to indicate the relationship between delving into things old and its relationship to the possession of knowledge. For generations historians, for example, assumed that Queen Boadicea issued no coinage. Recently an American businessman, whose hobby evidently involved numismatics – in particular Celtic coinage – corrected this erroneous concept *after thirty years of work.* He proved that while scholars had attributed the early silver 'boar/horse' coins to Antad, ruler of the Dubunni tribe, during the years 10 BC-AD 10, the last ancient British coins were struck to finance the Boadician Rebellion of AD 61.

Yet this stunning historical discovery hasn't caused the prices of ancient British coins to rise like leavened bread. Instead, as reported by the *Financial Times* of 19 September 1987, these coins have not enjoyed inherent appreciation to the extent that they might have. Indeed, specimens go for about half what the market reflected in 1970. Reasons given in the article for the lack of enthusiasm by buyers included: (a) discovery of rare examples by treasure hunters armed with metal detectors; (b) forgeries; (c) thefts from geological sites; and (d) sales from collections of deceased coin collectors.

Here at the end of the listing of reasons for the depressed prices of silver pieces of British history lies the key for the prospective silver trader who wants to participate in numismatics.

It has been estimated that by 1990 there will be more than 20 million people interested in numismatics. Not all of them, of course, will be interested in collecting silver coins. But those that do will probably specialise in specific areas such as American silver dollars; American silver coins other than dollars; Continental silver coins that could range from Greek silver drachmas to silver Austrian talers. There are also collectors of Japanese, Brazilian, Peruvian, Mexican, and British silver coins. But again, the collector who accumulates items of rarity may not be doing so simply to resell them at a future date and at a profit. As is so often the case, silver coin collections of numismatic worth are kept by collectors until death parts them from their beloved coins. And then the collection is auctioned off. In recent years, the prices paid for rare silver coins at auctions could cause their former owners to groan in the grave.

In the United States for some years there has been a tax benefit for collectors of silver and gold coins who upgrade their portfolios. The tax break here is that assuming a collector bought an interesting specimen of the 1561 Salzburg Jakob taler from the Credit Suisse Monetarium in Zurich for $350, held it for a year or so, and resold it for $600 – if the buyer of the taler upon its sale bought another silver coin at a price equal to or higher than the sold coin, no tax had to be paid on the profit from the resale. This is an aspect that has caused intense rising interest in numismatics by affluent Americans.

But for the silver trader who wants to make money on rare coins, semi-numismatic coins, or coins that could grow in value with the passage of time, the first thing that must be mastered is the ability to grade the coins being offered by a vendor, or to utilise the services of an expert who already knows how to grade these coins properly.

In this connection current coin-grading systems vary widely from those popular years ago, which were based on word descriptions such as 'fine', 'good' etc. Currently, a numerical grading system seems to be the most popular way of judging the conditions of a rare or numismatic coin. Table 2.3 details the various numbers assigned to MS (mint state) and lower grade coins.

Table 2.3 Numismatic coin grading table

Designation	Condition	Remarks
MS–70	Perfect uncirculated	Flawless and rather few
MS–65	Choice uncirculated	No sign of wear, some tiny nicks
MS–63	Select uncirculated	Called 'Brilliant uncirculated' More blemishes than MS–65
MS–60	Uncirculated	Coin may have spots, less lustre, some nicks or contact marks
AU–55	About uncirculated	Some wear on high points – with much of the mint lustre left
AU–50	About uncirculated	Wear on high points – and only half the original mint lustre left
EF–45	Choice extremely fine	Design details sharp – some lustre left
EF–45	Extremely fine	Design details sharp; high points flat – some lustre left; some wear
VF–35	Choice very fine	Design and lettering visible – and no lustre left; some wear
VF–30	Very fine	Major details visible; but wear heavy on high points; no lustre
F–12	Fine	Considerable wear; little detail on high points; main features clear
VG–8	Very good	Considerable wear; design recognisable
G–4	Good	Decorations, letters and design well-worn but recognisable

Source: The Metals Consultancy

The collector who intends to resell – and can afford the cost – would probably want to deal only in the best grade coins available. Since M-70 (perfect) coins are rather hard to come by, investments may have to be confined to the M-63 to M-65 areas of brilliant uncirculated specimens. The gradings above do not include proof coins, which today are issued in connection with the issuance of 'business strike' coins. Unlike the gradings of the coins listed above, proof coins are presumed to always be in museum-grade status since owners normally are not going to carry them about without cases protecting the coins. Struck twice to provide brilliance to the background and frosting to the high points of the coins, the proofs are technically perfect.

At this point in time, unlike banking and securities businesses in the United States, the coin business is still unregulated. So what it comes down to when seeking to buy or attempting to sell is that the trader has to pick a dealer to work with. Selecting a dealer who is to be trusted and performs in a satisfactory manner requires research and some digging. Finding experts who can help in acquiring an investment portfolio of silver numismatic coins may also be time consuming, but if the proper expert is found, the effort will prove worthwhile.

There is a myriad of periodicals and literature available for the prospective numismatist or trader on the subject of coins. These can range from *Coin World* in the *United States*, to *Coin & Medal News* in the UK, to *Australian Coin Review*, in Australia. Of course, there are numerous auctions held all over the world where collectors can buy and sell silver coins; and there are firms like R. M. Smythe & Co. in New York City that hold several 'mail-in' auctions each year. Many newspapers feature coin columns where new and interesting issues are announced. And there are annual publications that list relative values of existing numismatic and semi-numismatic coins.

Oscar Wilde once noted that experience is the name everyone gives to their mistakes. If the risk-taker invests in the superior grade coins of numismatic nature and holds them long enough the mistakes they may initially experience may turn out to be windfalls years later. But one mistake that must not be made is to amass a valuable coin collection and leave it around the house. It should be kept in a secure place – and handled rarely to avoid wear or scratching or blemishing.

3

TRADING IN PAPER SILVER

This is a milieu that relies upon the price of silver in world markets to generate increases or decreases in the equity inherent in the involved silver paper medium. Thus the trading medium could be a silver future, an option on a silver future, an option on a set amount of physical silver, a leverage contract on silver, or even equity shares in silver mining, refining and marketing companies.

To illustrate some of the facets involved in the world of paper silver, think back for a moment to the example cited in Chapter 1, where an investor had risked $75,000 to buy 10,000 ounces of silver at $7.50 an ounce and found his equity had increased $2,500 by a slight rise in the price of silver of 25 cents an ounce to $7.75. Assume that instead of taking the $75,000 and paying for the 10,000 silver ounces, the risk-taker had resorted to one of the forms or other in the silver paper world. If he had gone long in the New York futures market, he would have bought two COMEX silver futures of 5,000 ounces each – and depending on where the business was done would have put up anywhere from $3,000 to $5,000 per contract as initial margin. Since a future by definition is a contract to buy or sell a specific lot of the physical commodity involved in the contract at some time during a future month (at the option of the seller, not the buyer) it is understandable that the exchange member acting for the buyer requires a good-faith deposit professionally known as initial margin.

The exchange member carrying the trader's account would deposit the amount of initial margin required by the exchange. And thereafter would maintain the position according to the rise or the fall in the price of the involved future. Assuming the trader had gone long two December COMEX silver at $7.50 in October, and the 25 cent rise described occurred the following day, the exchange clearing house would have credited the account of the clearing member with $2,500. If a few days later silver stood at only $7.25, the trader's equity would have declined $2,500 and he would probably have been required to supply the decline of $2,500, which would have been sent to the clearing house to maintain the account's position. Since in the case of the example being illustrated the price advanced 25 cents above the market entry point of $7.50, the equity in the trader's account advanced by that much. Now if the trader desired to withdraw the equity increase, he could have asked for a cheque from the clearing broker, which would have been presented rather quickly with no interest or any other charges deducted or levied. And if the position advanced another 50 cents a few days later, the equity would have increased another $5,000 (50 cents times 10,000 ounces in the two 5,000-ounce contracts). The trader could have readily withdrawn this increase, or if the policy of the house where the silver contracts were held was to require an initial margin of $5,000, the trader naturally could have added another contract at the then entry price of $8.25, etc. Illustrative of the elements of a typical silver futures contract on COMEX is Fig. 3.1.

Continuing our assumed example of the trader who went long two December COMEX silver contracts and benefited by a one-day gain of 25 cents an ounce, upon inspection – and disregarding market entry commissions – the trader has a gross gain of $2,500 on a $10,000 deposit, or an advance of 25 per cent on the equity as compared to a 3.3 per cent advance for the risk-taker who paid in full for the 10,000 ounces in the previously mentioned physical silver transaction.

Conversely it must be realised that if the price of silver had declined 25 cents instead of advanced, the risk-taker who played with silver futures stood to lose 25 per cent of his $10,000 initial equity whilst the physical buyer had only a slight percentage loss. Moreover, if the futures position dropped by 50 cents, the trader would have to put up more maintenance margin (cash) to prevent being sold out. The physical buyer, of course, who had paid in full for the metal, owns it – whatever the going price may be – and cannot be sold out without that act being his decision.

The buyer of physical silver, who paid in full, lost the monetary use of the $75,000 required to pay for the 10,000 ounces at $7.50, but if that buyer had traded in the world of paper silver such money-use loss might have been avoided.

To illustrate this, assume the trader opened an account at a COMEX clearing member and deposited the entire $75,000 in his futures or commodity account (which, of course, are one and the same). That $75,000 would have been immediately put into Treasury bills (three months or six months as the account desired) which would have immediately started to earn a return on the deposit. Purchase of the two contracts – assuming the clearing member's house margin was $5,000

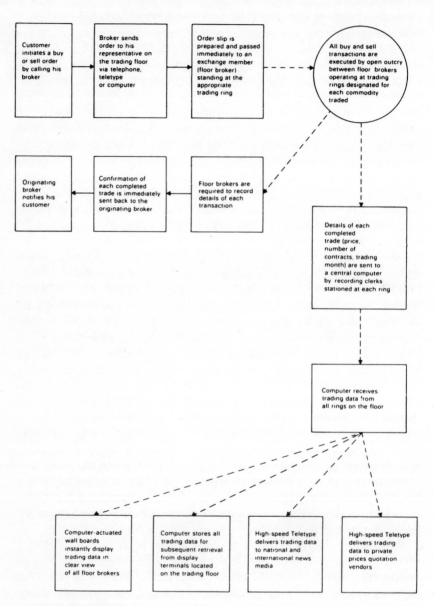

Source: New York Comex

Fig. 3.1 Elements of a typical silver futures contract

margin initially for each long future – would not have adversely affected the T-bill position, because the clearing member could deposit $10,000 in bills with the exchange clearing house as initial margin for the customer. His position, therefore, involved the two long silver futures contracts at $7.50, and concomitantly his $75,000 in T-bills were providing him a return on his money. Suppose then that the silver price declined and the account was asked for additional maintenance or as some firms call it 'variation' margin, the trader could instruct the broker to sell off enough bills to cover the margin call. On the other hand, if the price of silver increased and the equity in the account grew, the trader could use the increase in equity to (a) buy more T-bills; (b) add more silver futures to the position; or (c) simply withdraw the amount in excess of the required margin in the form of a cheque.

PAPER SILVER MARKETS

COMEX

COMEX, in New York, (Commodity Exchange) labels itself as 'the world's most active metals market'. This belief, in the thinking of its publicists, derives from the volume of 100-ounce gold and 5,000-ounce silver futures contracts traded in the pits each session. So that at the end of the trading year the statisticians come up with a vast number of silver contracts traded multiplied by 5,000 ounces and intimate that such a huge number of ounces passed hands during the trading year. Nothing could be further from the truth. COMEX, like other exchanges that trade in metal futures, permits holders of both long silver contracts and holders of short silver contracts to liquidate them by offset (making an opposite transaction: i.e. if long, a sale; and if short, a liquidating buy) at profits or losses (depending upon point of market entry). Indeed, research indicates that outside of the year of the silver situation (1979-80) more than 97 per cent of all COMEX silver contracts have been – and are – liquidated; without the metal ever being delivered by the seller to the buyer; and without the buyer ever having to pay for the metal involved in the future. Illustrative of this are the unusually large COMEX exchange stocks of silver on 31 October 1987 of about 150 million ounces. But the open interest (contracts remaining alive and not offset) on that same day stood at 82,890. Multiplying this number by 5,000, the result is 414,450,000 contracted silver ounces or about three times the available form and grade of silver approved by the exchange stored in exchange-approved warehouses.

Similar conditions prevail at other exchanges that trade in silver futures, such as the Chicago Board of Trade (CBOT), The Sydney Futures

Table 3.1 Principal silver futures exchanges and contracts*

COMEX
  4 World Trade Center, New York, New York 10048
  Phone: 212-938-2900
  Silver futures traded   *Trading hours*
  5,000 oz. silver   8:25 a.m. – 2:25 p.m. (NY time)

Chicago Board of Trade
  141 West Jackson Boulevard, Chicago Il. 60604
  Phone: 312-435-3500
  Silver futures traded   *Trading hours*
  1,000 oz. silver   7:25 a.m. – 1:25 p.m. (Chicago time)
  5,000 oz. silver   (In the Autumn of 1987 night trading began
                                             in these contracts. Contact the exchange to
                                             see if such activity still continues.)

MidAmerica Commodity Exchange
  175 West Jackson Boulevard, Chicago, Il.
  Phone: 312-435-0606
  Silver futures traded   *Trading hours*
  1,000 oz. silver   7:25 a.m. – 1:25 p.m. (Chicago time)

Tokyo Commodity Exchange for Industry
  Tosen Building, 10–8 Horidome, 1-Chome, Nihonbashi, Chuo-ku,
  Tokyo, Japan
  Silver futures traded
  10-kilos (320 oz.) silver   Minimum for delivery: 30-kilos

Sydney Futures Exchange
  Australia Square Tower (7th Floor), Sydney, 2000 Australia
  Phone: 02-241-1077
  Silver futures traded
  1,000 oz. silver

*Note: The most liquid silver futures contracts are on COMEX, followed by the Chicago exchanges.

Exchange. Table 3.1 details the exchanges where silver futures are currently traded.

London Metal Exchange

The world's largest 'terminal' market in silver is the London Metal Exchange (LME). It is both a paper market in addition to its role as a physical market in that contracts issued by LME members are negotiable at all times to the last day of the contracts called the 'prompt dates'. LME contracts (popularly called 'paper') cover lots of 10,000 troy ounces of silver. Basically there are two types of contracts, cash and forward.

LME cash contracts, which are due for delivery on the following day, must be backed by warehouse warrants. Like the warehouse certificates used in the rare cases of COMEX delivery, the LME warrants are negotiable and signify that approved LME metal is stored for the holder at an approved LME warehouse.

LME forward contracts are three-month delivery contracts which become cash contracts on the prompt date. Thus a forward contract issued by an LME member on 2 January 1988 would bear a 2 April prompt date – if that date was a day on which the exchange was open and conducted business. Until 1987 there was no clearing house and the LME contracts were settled between members.

A holder of LME silver warehouse warrants has readily negotiable collateral and can borrow on the silver stored in the warehouse. The amount that can be borrowed depends on the creditworthiness and character of the borrower. A trader who is long of forward silver contracts can resell them any time up to the prompt date simply by asking for the going price for that specific date. Since under normal conditions there is a contango (cash silver sells for less than the forward silver) between the cash market and the forward (three-month) market, the holder of a 2 April 1988 prompt date silver contract on 2 February will be quoted a lower price than the holder of a 2 May 1988 prompt contract because the period of the prior contract is thirty days less than the latter contract, and so on. Since contracts on the LME are for cash and for three months from the standpoint of pricing, members can 'take' a price off the three month price and issue contracts for longer periods (six months, a year, etc.). Although it is held to be not a futures market but instead a terminal market, where contracts in metals traded are satisfied by actual delivery and payment, the LME fulfils some of the requirements of a true futures market in that a holder of an LME contract can resell his contract, at a profit or loss, at any time to the prompt date, depending on point of market entry. Yet unlike organised futures exchanges elsewhere, clearing of contracts occurs between members rather than through a clearing-house. But since 1968, when silver began trading in the LME 'ring', cash contracts (24-hour delivery and settlement), and forward (three-month prompt) contracts are actively traded. Regular lots are of 10,000 ounces of silver, whilst job lots are less. Options on three-month silver are also available from members – and longer-term contracts and options may also be arranged by members with their clients – with the entry prices of the silver and the strike prices of the silver options 'taken off' the forward or three-month price. The London silver market fixing conducted in the offices of Mocatta and Goldsmid, bullion dealers to the Crown since the sixteenth century, impacts closely on the ring dealings in silver on the LME. But since there are a single silver fix in the bullion market and two morning and two afternoon ring-trading sessions for silver on the LME, it is understandable that the LME prices are affected by what goes on around the world with regard to silver trading, and LME ring prices for silver in their turn have an impact on the prices in both futures and physical markets all over the world. The prime reason that physical silver markets and paper silver markets remain aligned rather closely involves the fact that the leading bullion-trading members of the London silver market and the LME are interconnected with bullion trading and financing firms all over the world. Since London silver is traded in pounds sterling and New York and Chicago silver is traded in US dollars, chances for currency arbitrage arise from time to time, as do chances for arbitrage in the going prices of silver in London, New York and Hong Kong, for example.

LEVERAGE CONTRACTS

Bullion-dealing firms have for many years made long-term forward commercial deals with both silver producers and silver users. These forward contracts, also termed leverage contracts, were formerly restricted to commercial firms who bought and sold silver in some form or other. When the CFTC came into being in 1975 silver leverage contracts of a trade nature were beyond the scope and the power of that regulatory agency. As a result there were abuses of customers by some unregulated leverage contract dealers. But after years of public complaint and outcry the leverage contract industry in the United States became regulated by the Commodity Futures Trading Commission (CFTC), the US regulatory agency that supervises futures exchanges and registers future commission merchants, associated persons (brokers) and CTAs (Commodity trading advisers).

Today there are a handful of firms in America authorised to deal in these contracts, such as MONEX, of 4910 Birch Street, Newport Beach, California, 92660, which features leverage contracts on silver. MONEX have developed an approach where a trader or investor who believes silver will rise in price can go long and one who is of bearish opinion can go short. Because regulations require extensive disclosure statements and other materials which have to be read and signed if a risk-taker deigns to participate in physical silver – leveraged with only a 25 per cent deposit – it makes sense to send for a kit of the materials in order to get all the facts before taking market action one way or the other.

SILVER OPTIONS

By a silver option is meant the purchase for a money premium of the right to buy a set amount of silver (a silver call) or to sell a specific amount of silver (a silver put) at an agreed price (the strike price) up to (and usually including most of) a set death date (expiration date). There are two broad distinctions in the kinds of silver options actively traded: options on silver futures contracts; and options on physical silver.

The options on silver futures permit the holder of a call to acquire the subject future at any time up to and including the expiration date at the strike price from the account of the seller (hereinafter writer); whilst the holder of a put can deliver a silver future at any time up to the last day at the strike price to the writer. For example, if a risk-taker paid 20 cents an ounce premium for a December COMEX silver call struck at $8.00 on 14 October 1987, when the December future on that exchange traded at $7.79, the risk-taker cost would have been (before commission charges) $1,000 (20 cents times the 5,000 ounces in the contract). If the price of silver subsequently rose, the trader would make money on the $1,000. If it dropped, the most he could ever lose would be the $1,000. Thus the risk-taker who is bullish has the power of leverage ($1,000 controls the price action of $38,950) for a set length of time – and will never get a margin call, can never be liquidated without permission, and if possession is desired, can take delivery of the silver future involved in the call before expiration, position the future for a few weeks in his futures account and accept delivery during the spot month when the metal is tendered.

Conversely, the purchaser of a COMEX December silver put on 14 October 1987 struck at $7.75 and paying a premium of 20 cents an ounce has the right to sell to or deliver a silver future at that price, no matter how low silver might drop between the time of purchase and the second Friday of the previous month to the month on the option (a December option would expire on the second Friday of November, and so on).

In effect, the holder of a call on a silver future might be considered exactly in the same position as the owner of COMEX silver long contract – *without the downside risk*; and with all the upside benefits. In November 1986, when silver traded around $5.50, a $6 silver call for March went for about $300 (plus a small commission). The essential point is that whenever a trader decides the price of silver will rise, the most sensible way to approach the risk of being wrong is to buy exchange-traded silver calls. And for those who are bearishly inclined, the most sensible way of speculating in anticipation of a silver down-market is to purchase puts. If the market drops, the puts will generate fantastically leveraged downside profits. But if the exercise has been wrong and the silver price soars, the most the risk-taker can lose is the cost of the involved silver puts.

Exchange-traded options in the United States are exercisable in 'American style'. That is, the holders can exercise successful options at any time up to and including the expiration date. On the other hand in the physical and terminal markets of the silver world a goodly number of options are exercisable only in 'European style'. By this it is meant that the holder of the involved put or call can only exercise the involved option on the expiration date.

Silver options on 10,000-ounce lots are also available from LME members generally with European style of exercise. Silver trade options, that is to say options designed for commercial purposes (to place a ceiling on the silver price to be paid by a user when metal is needed; or to place a floor price under the market price of silver so a producing mine will wring a profit out of the ground no matter how far down the silver price may drop), are arranged by commercial firms with bullion dealers, bullion banks, and bullion brokers. Table 3.2 lists silver options traded at the time of writing.

Table 3.2 Principal exchange traded silver options*

COMEX	5,000 oz. options on silver futures traded on COMEX
Chicago Board of Trade	1,000 oz. options on the 1,000 oz. Chicago silver futures contracts
MidAmerica Commodity Exchange	1,000 oz. options on the MidAm silver futures contracts.

*Above contracts are options on silver futures. There are also exchange traded options on physical silver in much smaller quantities. But since these options trade in fairly illiquid markets, and since conditions of exercise are mainly European style (exercisable only on the last day of option life), the involved exchanges have not been listed. They do, however, include Toronto, Sao Paolo, Rio de Janeiro, and the European Options Exchange in Amsterdam.

SILVER SHARES

By definition a silver share is a share of equity stock in a company that has issued shares for public trading and whose primary activity involves, or depends on, the going price of silver. For example, one of the largest American silver mining companies, looking back into the past, has been Hecla Mining Company. The primary product mined by this company is an ore containing silver as a major ingredient. And so Hecla, even though it mines lead, zinc, rare earths and gold is considered a silver mining company. So is Sunshine Mining Company, Callahan, and Coeur de Alene Mines Corporation. Understandably, when the silver price plummeted toward $5 some years ago, most of these silver mining

Table 3.3 Leading American silver shares

Company	Where traded: leading activity	Price 21 January 1988
Asarco	NYSE; silver, base metals	21⅛
Callahan	NYSE; silver and gold	19⅜
Coeur d'Alene	AMEX; silver and gold	18
Hecla	NYSE; silver, gold, rare earths	13⅛
Sunshine Mining	NYSE; silver, gold, silver marketing	4⅛

Source: New York Times

companies went into gold also. The leading American silver mining companies are listed in alphabetical order in Table 3.3.

Since all the above companies have important operations in Idaho's fabled Silver Valley readers might be interested in seeing a listing of the volatile silver shares that trade on the Spokane Stock Exchange, Fig. 3.2.

Readers can write to the Spokane Stock Exchange, Spokane, Washington, for information on stocks listed on that exchange and to a regional broker in Spokane or Seattle Washington for information on stocks listed or under the rubric over-the-counter. 'Penny' silver stocks bought on the OTC market can sometimes make a nice profit for the smaller investor.

In addition to silver mining companies, and promotional silver mining companies that someday hope to mine if they can ever find financing when the silver price rises, there are fine companies listed on the NYSE and other exchanges that fabricate, refine and deal in silver in some form or other. Such companies include Engelhard, a publicly traded company that among other areas is prominent in silver and gold alloying and marketing; Handy & Harman, like Engelhard listed on the NYSE and involved in fabricating and marketing metals, including silver; Bank of Delaware, a bullion storage and lending bank; and Republic National Bank of New York, whose shares represent ownership not only of a well-run bank, but also of an aggressive bullion bank. And finally the Rhode Island Hospital Trust, which is probably the leading bullion bank in America. It is necessary to note that when silver runs up in price, past experience indicates that shares of companies involved in some form or other of silver activity move faster as the prices rise; and slower downward when the silver price reverses direction.

SILVER CERTIFICATES

By definition a silver certificate is a piece of paper attesting to represent a specified amount of silver on deposit at a bank or otherwise safe storage. For example, some years ago Mocatta Metals in New York, in order to

Trading in paper silver

SPOKANE STOCK EXCHANGE QUOTATIONS

LISTED STOCKS

Stock	Bid	Ask		Stock	Bid	Ask
Allied Sil	.37	.45		Nesco	.02	.04
ARI, Inc.	.70	.90		N. Hilarity	.03	0.6
Bio-Tech	4.50	5.00		Princeton	.09	.11
Callahan	20.50	21.50		Quad. Met.	.02	.04
Clayton Sil.	1.60	1.90		R. Apex Sil.	2.90	3.25
Cour	19.50	20.50		Silver Butte	.06	.09
Data Rite	.07	.10		Silver Cresc.	.08	.12
Gexa Gold	1.85	2.25		Silver Ledge	.03	.06
Gladstone	.10	.20		Silver Mtn.	.50	.55
Gold Coin	.42	.50		Sterl Svgs.	9.00	10.00
Gold Exprs.	.26	.30		Sunshine	4.10	4.50
Gold Res.	4.80	5.25		Thunder Mtn.	.85	1.05
Gold Sec.	.12	.14		Water Power	24.00	24.50
Grandview	.05	.07		Western Gold	.07	.12
Gulf Res.	13.00	13.75		Western Sil.	.18	.25
Hecla	13.50	14.25		West Sil. A	.17	.22
Helena Sil.	.05	.10		Yreka Unit	.08	.12
Homestake	16.75	17.75		**REGIONAL**		
Indep. Lead	.27	.30		U Sav Bk MT	6.00	6.75
Int'l B. Res.	.60	.90		Sec Fd Sav MT	4.50	5.25
L. Sq. Gold	.20	.30		First Fed (CDA)	5.75	7.50
Metaline Mng.	.02	.05		First Fed (MT)	6.25	7.00
Metropolit	.80	1.00		FNB of NI	14.50	17.00
Midn. Mines	.17	.22				
Mineral Mtn.	.08	.14				
Mnt. Prec. Mn.	2.20	2.60				

SPOKANE STOCK EXCHANGE QUOTATIONS

Silver	6.84	.07
Gold	480.40	3.50

OVER THE COUNTER

Stock	BID	ASKED		Stock	BID	ASKED
Aberdeen Id.	.20	.25		Lucky Three	.02	.05
Abot Mining	.45	.50		Mascot Sil.	.05	.08
Admiral	.01	.02		Merger	.22	.25
Alice Cons	.10	.20		Mines Mgmt.	.40	.60
Am. Placer	.01	.02		Nabob Sil.	.05	.08
Amazon Dixie	.20	.25		Nancy Lee	.19	.20
Amer. Silver	1.50	1.65		Nat'l Sil	.05	.10
Atlas	.25	.27		Nev. Stew.	.02	.04
Beacon Lite	.04	.06		Niag. Mng.	.30	.40
Bismarck	.15	.25		N. Am. Sil.	.15	.30
Bonanza Gold	.12	.18		Oom Paul	.13	.20
Burke Mng.	.07	.08		Painted Des.	.04	.08
Caledonia	.01	.02		Placer Crk.	.10	.15
Callah. Con	.25	.18		Plainview	.20	.25
Calnor Res.	.50	.75		Rock Creek	.25	.30
Canyon Sil.	.09	.12		St. Elmo Sil.	.15	.20
Capitol Sil.	.16	.20		Shosh. Sil.	.30	.40
Crs. Ind.	.13	.16		Sidney	.05	.06
Cen. Str. Gold	.06	.10		Sig. G. & Sil.	.02	.03
Cen. Sil.	.20	.30		Silver Beav.	.03	.05
Chp. Gold Sil.	.04	.08		Silver Belt	.10	.15
Chester	.45	.65		Silver Bowl	.07	.08
Chiwawa	.02	.05		Silver Buck	.16	.18
CDA Cresc.	.15	.20		Silver Cable	.10	.15
Conjecture	.20	.24		Sil. Corp. Am.	.03	.05
Con. Sil.	.80	.90		Silver Crest	.06	.10
Day Break M	.03	.05		Silver Cryst	.25	.50
East CDA	.03	.05		Silver Hill	.09	.12
East Star	.05	.08		Silver King	.08	.12
Emp. Expl.	.12	.20		Silver Ore	.06	.08
Evergreen	.06	.07		Silver Scot	.05	.10
Gold Bond	.10	.20		Silver Seal	.85	1.00
Gold Cache	.02	.05		Silver Secur	.03	.06
Gold Placer	.15	.20		Silver Star	.05	.08
Gold Res.	.02	.04		Silver Surp.	1.00	1.25
Gold Chest	.11	.18		Silver Trend	.03	.05
Golden Eagle	.02	.05		Square Deal	.10	.15
High Surp.	.30	.40		Sterl. Mng.	.50	.60
Hunter Crk.	.15	.16		Summit Sil.	.05	.10
Hypotheek	.07	.10		Sundance	.35	.40
Idaho Gen	.05	.10		Superior Sil.	.04	.08
Idaho Goldf.	.04	.05		Techsel. Inc.	.02	.04
Idaho Lead	.05	.10		United Mines	.03	.05
Id. Mon. Sil.	.04	.06		Ut. -Id. Con.	.01	.02
Idaho Sil.	.15	.20		Verde May	.12	.15
Inspir. Lead	.06	.07		Vindicator	.75	.85
Iron Mask	.03	.05		Virg. City	.01	.02
Judith Gold	.10	.15		W. Coast Trad.	.25	.40
Keystone Sil	.02	.03		West Strat.	.25	.40
King of Pine	.01	.02				
Lookout Mtn.	.01	.02				
Luc. Fri. Ex.	.16	.20				

Source: The Wallace Miner, Kellogg, Idaho, 14 January 1988

Fig. 3.2 Spokane traded stocks

aid customers who might fear that the United States would again confiscate the silver from its citizens as was the case in 1934, issued DOs (depository orders) – certificates purchasable through authorised Mocatta agents covering set amounts of silver stored in Switzerland and insured by Lloyd's of London against any calamity except two: nuclear war and market price deterioration. At the moment silver certificates are actively traded on the Montreal Exchange. This 'securitisation' of silver avoids sales and use taxes and the hassle of authentication on resale. As far as the author is aware, the Montreal traded silver certificates are the only exchange-traded silver certificates in the world. Investors, before buying or trading in these items, or in any storage certificates like Mocatta's DOs, should get full information about charges, commissions, and storage and insurance items.

Chapter 4 examines the strategies available to both short-term and long-term risk-takers in silver trading.

4

SILVER TRADING STRATEGIES

The first thing that prospective traders in silver must do is to familiarise themselves with the silver price. So before getting into silver up markets, silver down markets, or silver markets that fluctuate feebly, it is fitting to enlarge upon precisely what the silver price is.

On the last trading day in October 1987 LME silver closed in the following manner:

Cash or spot silver	pence 397.90...	$US 6.9550
3-months silver	406.95...	7.0885
6-months silver	415.80...	7.2220
12-months silver	433.25...	7.4990

On that very same day, COMEX silver futures ended up:

Spot month	$US 6.950
March 1988	7.136
May 1988	7.231
December 1988	7.592

At the end of that same trading session CBOT silver (in 1,000-ounce contracts) settled at:

Spot month (November 1987)	$US 6.94
February 1988	7.11
April 1988	7.20
December 1988	7.68

In the world of physical (cash) silver, here are the publicised prices at close of trading on 30 October 1987:

London silver market fixing (cash)	pence 401.40
3-months silver from cash price	410.85
6-months silver from cash price	420.30
12-months silver from cash price	438.60

On that same day the Handy & Harman base price for silver bullion stood at $US 6.95 per ounce, whilst Engelhard's price stood at $US 6.99.

A cursory glance at the above numbers reveals the following:

1   The price of silver is not quite the same in all markets.
2   Prices in American markets may differ from each other and from prices in London.
3   Prices in London may differ between silver prices in American markets, and also may differ between the publicised ones on the LME and the London silver market fixing.
4   In normal type markets reflected by the above prices, the farther out one goes in either the physical market for future delivery or in the futures markets months, the more expensive the market entry price is for the purchaser.

For example, a trader who is of bullish turn of mind and wanted to enter the COMEX silver futures market from the long side for a brief period of time, in early November, might select the December 1987 future, which on 30 October 1987 closed at $US 6.99 an ounce instead of the December 1988 COMEX future that, on 30 October, was $7.592. Theoretically this difference between delivery months in both futures and physical silver contracts is laid at the doorstep of the 'cost of carry'. In other words, it is assumed that somebody actually holds in storage the silver involved in futures and cash forward contracts. That is why the obvious differential between trading months in the futures markets of both silver and gold normally reflect the implied REPO rate. The differential between the months, professionally called the 'contango' changes with the changing price of silver and the going rates in the financial markets.

This sensitivity to price change caused by changing money rates, as well as by the laws of supply and demand from orders in the trading pits, understandably creates arbitrage and limited-risk opportunities for profits in silver trading. But before enlarging on this it is needful to note that a potential silver trader must at all times – during the trading sessions – not only be aware of markets he is involved in, or the markets he decides to risk funds in; but also be aware of the price action of silver in the major markets. Obviously then the active silver trader must have access to services such as Reuters Monitor and other services that the trader can utilise not only to retrieve silver prices as they change during trading sessions, but also the changes – if any – in the physicals markets of the world as displayed by bullion firms and brokerage firms with bullion-trading departments each day on screens like Reuters.

In Chapter 7, the factors that fundamentally impact upon the daily silver price are delineated; and in Chapter 8 the technical trading factors that influence the silver price up and down are elaborated. But at this point, an explanation of how the contango reacts and acts toward changes in interest rates and the silver price is germane:

● If interest rates rise, and the silver price rises, the contango between the months should theoretically increase.
● If interest rates remain the same, and the silver price rises, the contango between trading months should also rise.
● If interest rates fall, and the silver price declines, the contango between the months should theoretically lessen.
● If interest rates remain the same, and the silver price drops, the contango between the months should also decrease.

It is also necessary for a silver trader to know in which instances the contango helps or hurts a silver market position. Here is a listing of possible positions affected by the contango:

Silver position	Contango effect
Long future	hurts
Long call	hurts
Long put	helps
Long leverage contract	hurts
Long physical	hurts
Short future	helps
Short call	helps
Short put	hurts
Short leverage contract	helps
Short physical	helps

In this chapter so far, the silver price, as displayed in price discovery by futures and metal exchanges and by large bullion sources, has been touched upon. But what is the silver price for the small investor who may want to accumulate silver coins and/or small silver bars? Generally, legitimate sources, such as Sunshine Mining, which has a silver bullion division, will use the 'Handy' (the price publicised by Handy & Harman that is flashed each trading day to a waiting world at about noon, New York time). And in addition, as stated on page 5, the potential buyer of small bars is faced with payment of a fabrication charge. For the producer, such as primary silver mines, or mines that retrieve silver as a secondary product from base metals, or recyclers of silver, who glean funds from scrap, etc., the going silver price is generally again the Handy – with some variations. But in the final assessment, the silver price for small buyers is usually greater than the publicised prices on exchanges for spot silver; and upon resale, the small investor will probably receive a price reflecting a discount from the spot.

So what is the spot price?

While technically, the spot means the cash price reflected by the spot or cash month on futures exchanges as COMEX. This price is taken from the nearest active trading month, less the contango. For example, on 30 December 1987 COMEX spot and nearby active months traded:

	Open	High	Low	Close
Nov. (spot)	$696	$6.98	$6.96	$6.95
Dec. (spot)	$6.91	$7.08	$6.88	$6.99

Upon further inspection it appears that before that trading session only three 5,000-ounce silver contracts remained open on COMEX for the spot November delivery, whilst 36,661 contracts on 29 October were open for the most active COMEX contract, December 1987. It naturally follows that during COMEX trading sessions buyers and sellers of silver in physical form would have found the spot price offered them to follow closely the price pattern set up by trading in December 1987, the most active nearby COMEX month, rather than by November, the so-called spot month. Of course, legitimate vendors would have deducted the four-cent contango between the November and the December months at time of silver purchase or sale.

SILVER PRICE BOOM AND CRASH

Figure 4.1 is a bar chart of the silver price of the recent past. Chapter 8 has an explanation of the technical systems that help extend the volatile past into a profitable future for the trader. But at this point it suffices to use 20/20 hindsight and examine why the silver price took off for the stratosphere in 1979, climbed toward a $50 an ounce peak in early 1980, made a Matterhorn-like descent abruptly in March 1980 and has struggled ever since 1983.

Probably the most publicised – and most investigated commodity market event in American history – has been the so-called 'silver manipulation' or 'silver situation' of 1979-80. Yet despite intense investigation by the CFTC, Congressional hearings in both Senate and House in 1980, several books on the subject, reams of articles in financial media and even in a literary periodical like *Atlantic Monthly*, the findings in toto have still not been aired.

One significant finding that emerged, as the silver price rose during 1979 from about $6 towards the $25 level, involved the fact that some very wealthy Americans, Saudis, and sophisticated traders were silver buyers. Nothing was revealed to any great extent as to who were the sellers. When the outcry came from the trading pits that the buyers were attempting a 'silver squeeze' by taking delivery instead of liquidating existing open long positions, this generated sympathetic buying action,

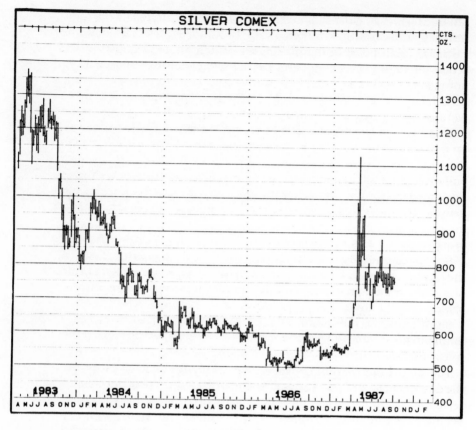

Fig. 4.1 Silver price 1983–87

causing upside price pressure on the shorts, as speculators joined the (as it turned out) rather ill-advised longs.

The major longs, who had established huge silver futures positions, at far lower prices than those ruling in the fall of 1979, understandably enjoyed their daily increases in equity caused by rising silver prices.

This happy state of affairs continued into the first week of January 1980, when exchange governors who were short – and hurting – did something drastic by not only raising margins on new and existing positions to record heights, but also by setting limits on the number of open contracts any speculator could hold in any single month and in all months combined on a net basis. Moreover, COMEX ruled that spot month trading could be only for liquidating purposes – no new positions. It did not take too long to foresee that the 'silver longs' would have to dump their positions in futures to the 'silver shorts' who had changed the rules. And even though these onerous changes should have caused a collapse of the silver price, it sagged gradually from $50 in January to about $34 at start of March 1980.

Part of the support to the silver price during this period came from action in the physicals market – especially London – where real silver, not paper, was being purchased by some of those forced to liquidate their long futures positions. And the physicals purchased, of course, were being pledged at banks in order to lever the purchases. Suddenly in mid-March 1980, the prime rate, then at about 15.5 per cent, shot up to (at that time) a record of 21.5 per cent *in one week*. And the then head of the Federal Reserve Board railed mightily at banks that had extended bullion loans to silver and gold speculators. A combination of a sudden rise in interest rates, coupled with an abrupt cancellation of bullion loans by banks created the kind of margin-call panic that was to prevail in the stock market in October 1987, when the Dow-Jones Index dropped over 500 points in a single session.

But back in the silver market, in the third week in March 1980 both the physical price and the futures price dropped towards the then nadir of $10.80 as the longs let go and the shorts laughed all the way to the bank.

Since that time the then leading silver longs have been branded as 'manipulators' whilst the exchange-member shorts, who changed the rules and broke the market, may still be laughing.

The silver price during the rest of 1980 managed to come back from the dead to head for $16 an ounce. And it might well have maintained its relatively traditional relationship to gold of about 33 to one if it hadn't been for the actions of the US Government, whose budget spokesman, David Stockman, decided that it made little sense for the Government to store 139.5 million silver ounces in the national stockpile. So in January 1981, when gold stood shakily at about $600 an ounce. and silver at about $16, the General Services Administration announced its intention to auction off the silver to help the incoming Reagan administration manage its budget. Naturally, Mr. Stockman, who had envisaged selling off the stockpile at a price of $15 or so, couldn't envisage the price-depressing effect of both the Government announcement and a campaign in February by at least one organisation whose primary role in life is to obtain cheap silver for its members. The Government announcement came even before the Reagan inauguration and in mid-February *Business Week* and other publications carried news that another 'silver bubble' was about to burst.

This initiated a down-trend in silver pricing that managed to catch its breath a bit toward the $10 level, sinking in 1982, when the General Services Administration indeed finally managed to hold some silver auctions down to the $8 level. Thereafter, dismal industrial conditions, lack of promotion of silver as a precious metal by producers while the clamour for cheap silver remained unabated by the silver users, brought the price down to just below the $5 an ounce level in 1986. As indicated in Figure 4.1 the silver price stagnated between $5.50 and $6 from the summer of 1986 through the February of 1987.

In the spring of 1987, interest in silver again began growing – with aggressive marketing of silver coins during the last few months of 1986, and the realisation by astute investors that the ridiculously wide gold/silver ratio of over 75 to 1 meant that silver was greatly undervalued to gold. These favourably bullish factors once again began to attract small and large investors into buying silver in some form for future appreciation. News of Chinese silver buying assisted the silver price to leap suddenly from under $5 an ounce to over $11, when again it was set back by strong professional selling of silver futures during the absence of bullish private speculators. At the time of writing, the silver price is between $6 and $7 an ounce and may be on the rise.

In this connection, here are some speculator/trader strategies suggested by diverse risk-taker points of view of silver market behaviour in the future. Strategies for hedgers will be found in Chapter 5.

Silver price rise

Inventory status	Strongly bullish	Mildly bullish
1 Long silver physicals	add to inventory or buy calls	do nothing
2 Long silver futures	add to position or buy calls	raise sell/stops
3 Long silver calls	add to position buy more calls	write calls
4 Short silver puts	sell more puts	buy protection
5 Idle cash	sell naked puts	do nothing
6 Long silver leverage contracts	add calls	sell leverages

1 *Long silver physicals*: It is suggested that if serious trading is intended involving physical silver, that silver in amount, and of purity and form acceptable to operating futures exchanges such as COMEX (5,000 ounces in standard bars), Chicago Board of Trade (1,000 ounces and 5,000 ounces). LME (10,000) be considered as 'inventory'. In this regard, the owner of such silver has the flexibility to act quickly in any situation. For example, if physical silver of say 5,000 ounces is all paid for, the owner can readily accumulate another 5,000 of physicals by putting up the warehouse receipt with a bullion bank or lending source. Also upon sale, the physical silver owner of exchange-grade silver can quickly receive the proceeds of a sales transaction. Assuming that the risk-taker is strongly bullish then more physical silver can be acquired.

Or if sensibly desiring limited risk re the new acquisition, the speculator can instead purchase one or more silver calls.

If the expectations of the owner of physical silver are only mildly bullish it is suggested that nothing be done. Before making a market decision the trader must be utterly convinced of the direction of the market. If only lukewarm expectations arise as to the immediate direction of the silver price, it's best to just stand aside and do nothing.

2 *Long silver futures*: Strong bullish sentiment calls for increasing the existing long futures position either with additional long futures positions or by purchase of additional call options on silver futures. Calls on 5,000-ounce COMEX futures are available from any COMEX member serving the public; and calls on 1,000-ounce CBOT silver futures are available from CBOT members dealing with the public. The sensibility of adding calls to existing futures positions is that if the risk-taker is wrong, and the anticipated strong price rise does not occur; but instead a setback depresses prices, then the most that can be lost is the involved call premiums. In other words, whilst the holder of long futures may reap fantastic benefits with the calls added, if right; the aspect of margin calls and severe losses over and above the original position held in the futures – if wrong – is absent.

If the holder of long silver futures is only mildly bullish, he may be wise to enter stop/sell orders in the event that the silver price declines instead of rises. If the silver price indeed appreciates somewhat and the holder of the futures position is still only mildly bullish then a protective stop could be raised in case the brief rally in the market goes into reverse.

3 *Long silver calls*: If already long calls on silver futures, the risk-taker, who is strongly bullish, should average upward by buying more calls. It may be held that the buyer of a silver call is similar to the holder of a long silver futures contract – without the downside risk. By averaging up in this fashion he avoids the financial headaches and heartaches that come from the need to supply variation margin if the silver price reverses.

If the holder of long silver calls is only mildly bullish it might profit him or her to write or sell silver calls at higher strike prices than the ones in portfolio.

4 *Short silver puts*: If expectations are strongly bullish, the risk-taker can enlarge the position by selling further puts. The seller of such puts is similar to holders of long futures if the price drops. But if it rises, the puts will deteriorate in value or die and the seller will profit thereby. This, of course, enlarges the downside risk. But after all, the trader has to have faith in his expectations.

If the trader is only mildly bullish it might make sense to buy some protection to the existing position by buying protective puts.

5 *Idle cash*: If the risk-taker entertains expectations of a strong advance in the silver price a sensible strategy instead of rushing in to buy physical silver, or pay premiums for silver calls, or position silver leverage contracts, is to simply write (sell) silver puts. If the market rises, the seller will profit from the premiums earned since the puts will expire. If the market instead drops, the risk-taker will have bought the silver futures involved in the puts at less than they were going for at the time the silver puts were sold.

Should the possessor of idle cash not feel strongly about a forthcoming silver price rise, then nothing need be done in the silver market, and the idle cash can be put to work earning something from T-bills, gilts, shares of $1 constant money market funds, or whatever, which can be liquidated quickly when cash is needed.

6 *Long silver leverage contracts*: If strongly bullish and long of silver leverage contracts that are appreciating in value, the holder might be more prudent if he or she added silver call options to the portfolio instead of adding more leverage contracts. Profits will grow if the silver does go up strongly, but potential losses are limited only to the costs of the added calls – and, of course, in the already at-risk leveraged position. If the holder of successful silver leverage contracts doesn't anticipate a strong upside move in the silver price, he or she might think about selling leverage contracts against the ones already owned.

Having touched upon the bullish-oriented silver trader it is now time to suggest something for the silver bears.

	Silver price fall	
Inventory status	Brutally bearish	Mildly bearish
1 Short physical silver	add to position	do nothing
2 Short silver futures	add shorts or buy puts	buy calls
3 Long silver puts	buy more puts	buy calls
4 Short naked calls	sell more naked calls	buy calls
5 Idle cash	Short futures/buy puts	do nothing
		buy calls
6 Short leverage contracts	Buy puts	do nothing
		buy calls

1 *Short physical silver*: Since the physical markets generally require 24-hour delivery of presold cash metal, the short-seller has to be able to borrow or lease silver from a bullion source, hopefully to replace the metal by purchase in the market when the silver price drops. Thus shorts in physical silver are not the normal speculator/risk-taker. Instead they are probably involved in some aspect of the bullion business. And if

brutally bearish in conviction – and if the silver is available for borrowing at sensible terms – and if willing to take increased risks, then the short-seller can add to his existing physical short position.

If only mildly expecting a price decline, or to put it in another light, if expecting only a mild decline, the bearish physical silver short might be well advised to simply do nothing.

2 *Short silver futures*: Generally the same original (initial) margin deposits rule on the various exchanges for longs in silver as well as shorts. And when the silver price encounters increased volatility, it has been the custom of the silver-trading futures exchanges to suddenly raise the margins (retroactively). Since the shorts in silver are, of course, aided by the existence of the contango (if the silver price remains stagnant the far out months gradually fall in price as they turn into the nearby ones), chances are the majority of the shorts on the exchanges are either the 'trade' (meaning the bullion business) or the floor (meaning the 'locals'). I am convinced that the silver bears among public speculators were wiped out pretty well during the 1979 early-1980 fiasco; just as so many silver bulls have been wiped out by the long decline in the price since 1980. In any event, the bear, who is short futures and who is utterly convinced there will be a price collapse before his position in open futures enters the spot month, can increase the existing risk by adding more short positions. Or perhaps more sensibly can simply buy some silver puts. In this manner the risk-taker is limiting the danger of upside risks to the costs of the puts.

If the risk-taker is only mildly bearish, the trader actually may have unexpressed second thoughts about the market; and it might make sense for him to go long some silver calls to protect the open short positions in the silver futures.

3 *Long silver puts*: If the trader is dedicated to a bearish posture with limited risk through the purchase of silver puts, and is convinced there will be a further decline, his most obvious strategy is to buy more puts. If he's wrong, the most that can ever be lost is the cost of the purchased options.

Supposing the trader is only mildly bearish, and already has a profitable position in silver puts, it might be wise for him to lock in some of the paper profits by purchasing silver calls.

4 *Short naked calls*: The rules of the exchanges listing silver puts and calls for trading permit a speculator, as well as a professional market-maker or bullion source, to sell uncovered or naked calls and puts. By this is meant that if the option silver seller is short a silver future and sells a silver put against the short future, he is 'covered'. If the option-seller sells the put without a covering short position in the future, he is uncovered, or 'naked'. Conversely, if the trader is long a silver future

and sells a call against the position, he is covered. And if he sells a call against a cash deposit instead of a long future contract, the seller is considered naked or uncovered. Actually the seller of a naked call is considered in the same light as a trader who is short a silver future. Thus the thrust of this strategy in a declining silver market is to sell naked calls and earn the premiums paid as rewards for the risks assumed.

So if the risk-taker already is naked, he or she might want to add to the existing position – if convinced the silver market would drop significantly in price.

If the naked call seller has a profitable position and is only mildly bearish in market expectations, the trader might be wise to buy some protective calls.

5 *Idle cash*: Of all the available strategies for a dedicated silver bear with money to risk, the purchase of silver puts appears the most attractive. Only by buying puts, which have been held by some as simply bets that the silver market will drop – and no one can lose more than the costs of those bets, if wrong – can a trader approach downside silver profits with absolutely limited risk.

If the trader is only mildly expectant of a silver price decline, the chances are that the idle money can be put to better use elsewhere, possibly even in investments in the tremendously depressed equities markets around the globe.

6 *Short leverage contracts*: According to officials at MONEX, interest is paid to short-sellers of their leverage contracts. Since these contracts increase in equity for the shorts if the silver price declines, should the shorts be convinced that there will be a continuous decline in the silver price, they might add to their existing risks by putting on additional short silver leverage contracts. Or since MONEX also vends silver puts and calls, the risk-taker might want to limit risk on additional short leverage contracts and instead purchase silver puts on physicals from MONEX.

If the risk-taker is not convinced silver will do anything else but simply mildly decline before the price shoots up again, he could either do nothing, or perhaps purchase some protective silver calls from MONEX to lock-in profitable short-leveraged positions.

SILVER SPREADING

Strategies for trading in silver markets not only include the few major items for bullish and bearish speculators listed above, they also include the following:
1 Spreads in futures which are bullish or bearish.
2 Spreads in options on silver futures, which are bullish or bearish.

3   Combinations employing physicals, futures, options and/or leverage
     contracts.
4   Market-straddling techniques that bring profits no matter which
     way the silver market goes – as long as it goes.

Spreads in silver futures

Essentially a silver futures spread consists of going long one delivery
month and simultaneously going short a different delivery month.
Being long and short of silver futures at the same time, of course, limits
profit horizons, but concomitantly limits capital risk, since silver futures
of varying months rise and fall in sympathy with the rise and fall of the
silver price. But because of the factors influencing the contango,
mentioned earlier in this chapter, and because of conditions of buy and
sell orders in the pits for the various silver futures delivery months, the
fall and rise of each silver futures month in accord with the fall and rise
of the silver price may not be quite the same.

That is why the silver spreaders have to have expectations as to
whether the differential between the trading months selected will
widen or narrow in the foreseeable future.

In the case of the bullish spreader, the nearby month is sold short and
the farther out month is positioned long. For example, the trader might,
in November 1987, sell short the July 1988 and simultaneously go long
the December 1988 silver future. Obviously this spreader believes the
contango will widen with an increased silver price next year – and
if so the loss on the July short will be less than the gain on the
December long. So that net of charges, the bullish silver spreader
anticipates a profit. Since a spread position is not as risky as either a
straight short or long future, the margin required is far less for the
spread. Before putting on any silver spreads it is suggested that the
margins at the clearing member where the business is to be conducted
be determined; and the transactions charges discovered before doing
the business.

In the case of the bearish silver futures spreader, the reverse of the
bullish manoeuvre occurs. Here the nearby month is purchased and the
farther out month sold short. So the bear spreader in November 1987
might go long the July 1988 silver future and simultaneously go short
the December 1988 delivery month. In this instance, of course, the
spreader hopes that a declining silver price will result in a narrowing of
the spread so that the profit on the December short will exceed the loss
on the July future and the accompanying costs of putting the spread on
and unwinding it later.

Spreading with options on silver futures

There are many kinds of silver futures options spreads, including vertical, horizontal, and butterfly spreads. There are bullish vertical spreads and bearish vertical spreads, for example. And some innovative traders have even ventured into diagonals. But in its simplest form, the option on silver futures spread involves two calls or two puts. Silver options, like listed options on other commodities and securities, are struck at varing price levels with reference to the current markets. For example, with spot silver between $6.50 and $7.00 a potential spreader can find puts and calls whose strike price (contract price) is, say at $6.25; $6.50; $6.75; $7.00. Assuming the future to be optioned is trading at $6.75, the call option struck at $6.75 is 'at-market'; the one struck at $6.50 is 'in-the-money'; the call option trading at a $7.00 strike is 'out-of-the-money'. With this bit of background, consider some of the spreading possibilities with options on silver futures contracts.

Market expectations	Type of option spread
1 Bullish	Vertical call bull spread
	Vertical put bull spread
2 Bearish	Vertical put bear spread
	Vertical call bear spread
3 Stable	Horizontal calendar call spread
	Horizontal calendar put spread

1   Bullish vertical call spread involves purchase of an at-market or in-the-money silver call and simultaneous sale of a silver call for the same delivery month struck at a higher level than the call purchased. For example, in November 1987 a bullish option spreader could go long (buy) a March 1988 COMEX $7.00 call and simultaneously go short (sell) a March 1988 COMEX $7.50 call. Understandably the most the trader can profit, if silver rises beyond $7.50 an ounce during the life of the call is 50 cents an ounce on the 5,000 ounce option, or $2,500, less the premium differences and the transaction charges. But how much does the risk-taker stand to lose if the silver price stays still or declines under $7? The answer is the monetary differential between what the trader had to pay for the lower-struck call and what was received from the sale of the higher-struck call, and the transaction charges.

In converse manner, a bullish put spreader would sell a higher strike put of the same expiration month and simultaneously buy an in-the-money or at-market put. As will be explained in Chapter 6, this type of spread unlike the vertical call bull spread requires margin deposit. But in effect if the price of silver should rise above the strikes of both puts, the most the spreader can gain from the rise is the differential in the strikes plus the credit over and above transaction charges ensuing from the premium differentials.

2   In the case of the bearishly inclined trader who wants to employ spreads in down markets, the vertical put bear spread calls for purchase of an at-market or in-the-money put and the simultaneous sale of a put for the same delivery at a lower strike price than that of the purchased put. For example, in November 1988 the trader might buy a $7 March 1988 COMEX silver put and simultaneously go short (sell) a March $6.75 put. If the market does decline the most the spreader can earn is the differential in the strike prices less the transaction charges and the premium differences upon entry into the spread.

Since an at-market or in-the-money call demands a higher money premium upon purchase than calls trading away from the market and thus out-of-the-money, bearishly inclined spreaders can go long an out-of-the-money call and simultaneously for the same delivery month sell short an at-market or in-the-money call. If the silver market indeed declines so that both calls will expire (a polite way of saying 'die'), then the most that the bearish spreader can earn is the differential between the call strikes and the residue of the premium credit after transaction charges at the outset. And as is the case with the bullish trader who uses puts to make money in a rising market, the bearish spreader who uses calls to make money in a falling market will be asked to put up margin. This too will be explained in Chapter 6.

3   In stable markets silver option spread traders hope to profit upon changes in the premiums relative to the market assessment of the time or extrinsic value in the involved options. In this regard the spreader can use either two calls or two puts with the same strike prices but differing expirations. For example, a spreader in November might go long a May $7 COMEX silver call and simultaneously go short a March $7 call. Possible profit ensues as the March call approaches expiration and the premium for the time left in the $7 May call exceeds the original debit entailed in the spread. Since the spreader buys the call at the same strike with a longer expiration date than the one that is sold short, no margin is required. On the other hand, if the spreader believes he can profit from buying the March $7 call and simultaneously selling the May $7 call, then this type of calendar spread does require margin, as will be explained in Chapter 6.

The calendar spreader can buy, instead of calls, puts in pursuit of the same kind of extrinsic goals. In this case, if the May $7 COMEX silver put were purchased and the March $7 put simultaneously sold, no margin would be required outside the premium differentials, which would normally be a debit to the spreader. Conversely the spreader could buy the March $7 COMEX put and simultaneously sell the May at the same strike, garnering a possible credit from the premiums. But here the spreader would have to put up margin as explained in Chapter 6.

Combination spreading

Welcome to the world of butterflies, conversions, boxes, and other innovative strategies that could involve combinations of silver options by themselves; silver futures and options on silver futures; silver physicals and silver futures and silver options; and innovative market attempts to come ahead when spread by virtue of low-cost transaction fees, such as those available to floor members and clearing members of exchanges such as COMEX, CBOT and others that trade in paper silver media. Since this book is primarily slanted toward the speculator/trader who may not be an exchange member these professional strategies will not be delved into in great detail; but merely posed by way of information to assist potential silver traders in understanding the possibilities that exist in the busy silver pits with futures, physicals and options.

1 *Vertical butterflies* are characterised by purchase of two calls and simultaneous sale of two other calls. For example, if March silver traded at $6.50, a spreader could buy one March $6.25 silver call and one March $6.75 call, whilst simultaneously selling two March $6.50 calls – if the premiums received for the sale of the two short $6.50 calls exceed the premiums paid for the in-the-money $6.25 call and the out-of-the-money $6.75. The rule for making this kind of butterfly therefore simply is that the distance between the purchased strikes and the strikes of the short calls must always be equal (i.e. 25 cent intervals or 50 cent intervals, and so forth); the expiration months of both the long calls and the short calls must be the same; and the excess in the premiums over the transaction costs must make sense. In similar manner, the butterfly maker might try it with puts instead of calls. In this instance, of course, the spreader would go long two puts and sell two other puts. For example, if March silver on COMEX traded at $6.50, the spreader could buy one $6.75 silver put and one $6.25 put, whilst simultaneously selling two $6.50 puts. In both cases, the vertical call butterfly and the vertical put butterfly, the spreader – if he can manage a net premium over in-and-out charges – cannot lose any capital, no matter which way the silver market goes during the term of the involved options.

2 *Horizontal butterflies*, like the vertical species, involve four options: two calls bought and two calls sold; or two puts bought and two puts sold. If March silver traded on COMEX at $6.50, the spreader could go long a March $6.50 call and a July $6.50 call, whilst simultaneously

selling short two May $6.50 calls. Or he could go long a March $6.50 put, and a July $6.50 put and simultaneously go short two May $6.50 puts – again in either case if the premiums received for the sale of the two middle term options exceeded the cost of buying the nearer-term option and the further out one. Thus the horizontal butterfly rule is that the strike prices on all the involved options be the same and the distance between the near-term and the middle-term be precisely the same time interval as the time between the mid-term and the further out options. There also exists the more complex possibilities of diagonal butterflies which there isn't space to discuss here.

3 *Conversions*: In this frequently used manoeuvre, puts on silver are used to create calls and calls are used to create puts. In order to accomplish this, the trader must also simultaneously go long or short silver futures. For example, a demand arises in the pits for a $6.50 March silver call. Now assume that silver delivery month is quietly trading at that level; but no calls are being offered because traders envisage a surge in the silver price. And some of those believers are offering $6.50 March puts. The trader who wants to create a call buys a $6.50 put and simultaneously goes long the March future at $6.50 and also at the same time sells the $6.50 call to the unknown buyer. This is done if the trader can come out with a profit over transactions costs from the premium received for the sale of the call. Conversely if the silver market looks weak and the demand is for March $6.50 puts but only $6.50 calls are being offered, the trader can buy the proferred call, simultaneously go short the March future at $6.50, and sell a 'covered' put to the unknown buyer. Notice that in the conversion process, where a put became a call, and the reverse of that where a call became a put, the trader assumes no risk at all, since in the first instance the positioned long future that is held to cover the short call is protected by the purchased put, if the market declines, the call dies, and there is a drop in value of the positioned long future. Any decline in that direction is offset by a like appreciation in the protective put. The same is true in the case of the short future used to cover the vended put. If the market rises and the short future grows a loss on paper, the protective purchased call will increase similarly in value.

Thus the trader who is involved in the conversion or reverse conversion process has to be content with the small profit achieved when the conversion or reverse conversion came into being. That profit is limited to the excess of the premium received over the premium expended and the transaction costs.

4 *Straddling*, a manoeuvre applicable to volatile silver markets, involves the simultaneous purchase of a silver put and a silver call at about the same strike price for the same or differing expiration months.

For example, with spot silver at $6.95 on 30 October 1987, a risk-taker expecting unusual volatility (up or down) in the near-term silver price could have purchased a $7 March 1988 silver call and a $7 March 1988 silver put for a combined premium of $1.16 an ounce (before commissions). Now if silver rose more than say $1.25 an ounce prior to the call option expiration, or dropped over $1.25 from the $7 strike level of the put portion of the straddle, the risk-taker would begin to make money. And it follows that if the price range during that period fell somewhere between $8.25 and $5.75 the risk-taker would recover some of his investment. In the rather rare instance where the silver price would be precisely at $7 during the life of the options, there would be no chance for recovery of any of the involved costs. But before entering into any straddle purchase at a fixed price, analysis of the premiums and conclusions about market direction and volatility during the term of the options contemplated must be done by the risk-taker.

That is why some straddlers instead of buying both a $7 March call and a $7 March put on 30 October 1987 might have opted for a straddle with differing strike prices. For example, a $7.25 March call on that date went for 57 cents, whilst a $6.75 March put sold for 40.5 cents, or a gross cost for this combination of 97.5 cents. Here the purchaser would have a savings in premium of 27.5 cents in return for sacrificing 25 cents.

SILVER OPTION WRITING (SELLING)

Up to this point the various market strategies suggested for varying price movement conditions has basically involved buying physical silver, silver futures, silver options on futures, etc. When a speculator is faced with the problem of attempting to make profits in a market dominated by professional traders and hedgers, *buying* options (puts, calls or straddles) seems the most sensible approach since all the risk is relegated to the cost of the options. If the trader is wrong and the market is unfavourable in direction to the purchased options, then the most that can be lost are the fixed – and prepaid – sums involved in the option purchases. So it may be rightfully held that the buyer of a silver option seeks profits with all the risk known and fixed at the time of market action, whilst the option seller (or as some professionals term that worthy, the option writer) receives all the possible gain at time of acceptance of the premium – and thereafter is subjected to unknown, and in some case unlimited risk. Table 4.1 delineates the market position of both silver exchange traded option buyers and sellers.

Table 4.1 Risk/reward silver option buyers/sellers

Situation	Market rise	Market drop	Risk	Reward
Long call	value up	value down	loss of cost	unlimited
Long put	value down	value up	loss of cost	unlimited
Long straddle	call value up	put value up	loss of cost	unlimited
	put value down	call value down		
Short call	call value up	call value down	unlimited	limited
(covered)			to future	to premium
Short call	call value up	call value down	unlimited	limited to
				premium
Short put	put value down	put value up	unlimited	limited to
(covered)			to short future	premium
Short straddle*	Call value up	put value up	unlimited	limited to
(naked)	put value down	call value down		premium

Source: The Metals Consultancy
Note: When the strikes in a straddle are not the same, but are far apart (i.e. the silver call struck at $7.50: the put at $6.50, instead of both at $7 as in a straddle, the combination is called a 'strangle'. Of course a straddle or a strangle can be written (sold) naked, partly covered, or even covered, as the case may be).

TRADING PLANS

Before even thinking about trading the volatile silver markets for profits in any of their diverse aspects, the risk-taker should construct a trading plan. This should include (a) limits to financial commitment; (b) planned points of market entry and exit: (c) preplanned stop-loss and profit areas.

The trader should maintain an account with an exchange member, member or associate member of an international physical market in order to have order-execution capability in more than one trading arena.

The potential silver trader should know the fundamentals of silver supply/demand; and be versed in a workable system of charting or some other technical aspects of price, volume and open-interest movements and their effect on silver prices. As will be seen in Chapter 8 (Silver technical research) charts of any kind are reflections of the past supposed to provide signals for what can only be an uncertain future. But they do help traders arrive at buy and sell decisions.

Execution of a well-structured trading plan requires both discipline and flexibility. Such discipline includes keeping successful silver market positions to a planned maximum, for example; and flexibility requires alteration of a rigid trading plan when market conditions change.

Finally, consider the advantages of buying options to any other silver market strategy. Thus if the risk-taker decides the market could rise within a certain time period, he or she should buy silver calls – either physical or calls on futures. If the market drops instead of rises, there are no margin calls; and the trader already knows how much he may lose at the time of call purchase. Conversely, if the trader is bearish and thinks silver should go down within a specified time period, the trader would be better off buying puts instead of going short physicals or futures or leverage contracts. In this case, if the market soars instead of drops, the trader who owns puts will lose only what the puts cost. The trader who is short futures or silver leverages contracts can never be sure precisely how much will be lost if silver takes off again for fundamental reasons.

5

SILVER HEDGING STRATEGIES

Although the dictionary offers diverse meanings for the term 'hedge', when it comes to silver a hedge means a device to shift price risk from the owner, and/or the short-seller, of silver in physical or paper form to somebody else. Basically there are silver buying and silver selling hedges.

In this connection, a silver mining management may want to make sure there is a floor sales price under the silver they will be mining in the future; and a silver user may desire a ceiling or 'cap' purchase price the user will be paying for future silver. Silver traders and speculators can also shift their risks by placing floors against deterioration during price drops in long positions in physicals and/or silver futures and options; or ceilings to protect from price rises in short silver physicals and/or paper positions. Hedging is costly – and since its purpose is basically price insurance that expense must be considered in the light of future price expectations.

SILVER POSITIONS AND POSSIBLE HEDGES

The hedging media available to silver producers, users, and speculators or traders are silver futures and silver options, in the main. Silver leverage contracts may also be used as hedges in situations parallelling those of silver futures. Since silver futures, their prices, volume and open interest are openly displayed in the financial press, they are suggested in the table that follows. But silver leverage contracts may be considered the equivalent of strategies involving futures. Table 5.1 lists theoretical silver-risk positions and the results of applying available hedging instruments to them.

By way of further clarification of the items in the above table it is best to take each of the ten trading situations and the twenty hedging possibilities for those ten categories and expand on them.

Silver hedging strategies

Table 5.1 Silver positions and possible hedges

Silver position	Hedge medium	Strategy	Result
1. Inventory	Future	Short future	Protected vs drop (locked in)
2. Inventory	Option	Buy put	Protected vs drop (not locked in)
3. Long future	Future	Short back mo.	Protected vs drop (locked in)
4. Long future	Option	Buy put	Protected vs drop (not locked in)
5. Long call	Future	Short future	Protected vs drop (locked in)
6. Long call	Option	Buy put	Protected vs drop (not locked in)
7. Long put	Future	Buy future	Protected vs rise (locked in)
8. Long put	Option	Buy call	Protected vs rise (not locked in)
9. Future inventory	Future	Long future	Protected vs rise (locked in)
10. Future inventory	Option	Buy call	Protected vs rise (not locked in)
11. Short physical	Future	Long future	Protected vs rise (locked in)
12. Short physical	Option	Buy call	Protected vs rise (not locked in)
13. Short future	Future	Long back mo.	Protected vs rise (locked in)
14. Short future	Option	Buy call	Protected vs rise (not locked in)
15. Short call	Future	Long future	Protected vs rise (locked in)
16. Short call	Option	Buy call	Protected vs rise (not locked in)
17. Short put	Future	Short future	Protected vs drop (locked in)
18. Short put	Option	Buy put	Protected vs drop (not locked in)
19. Future sale inv.	Future	Short future	Protected vs drop (locked in)
20. Future sale inv.	Option	Buy put	Protected vs drop (not locked in)

Source: The Metals Consultancy
Note: Wherever the word future is used in the above table, it may be substituted with the words 'leverage contract'. And wherever the words 'option', 'put' and 'call' are used, the hedger can hold these terms to mean either options on futures or on silver physicals.

1 *Inventory* (future): In this instance, the potential hedger owns actual silver and desires to protect the metal from price deterioration for a specific time period. If the future is chosen as the hedge instrument, the strategy would be to go short the silver future of the delivery month where the hedger feels the protection may no longer be needed. If the silver market drops during this period, the loss on the cash-market value of the physical silver in inventory should approximate the gain in equity on the short silver future position. There are several obvious disadvantages to this type of protective price hedge: (a) if the price of silver rises during the time the silver source is short, additional variation margin may be required; and (b) if the price of silver does not drop but instead rises, the hedger who is short the future is locked-in, since whatever might be gained by the appreciation in the physical position because of a market price rise is obviously lost in the worsening of the short futures position.

2 *Inventory* (option): In this case the owner of physical silver would purchase put options to protect the physicals from price drops during the life of those options. Here the hedger expends money for the protection in the form of put premiums; but understandably the silver owner is not locked in, as in the case of hedging with a short future. If the silver price rises, the value of the physical inventory will also rise. But the protective put, of course, will erode in value – only in extent to its cost. Thereafter, the owner of the inventory, who has used purchased puts for protection, can reap the benefits of a market gain, while he has had the peace of mind that his protected floor price for his silver holdings were the strike price of the puts, minus their costs.

3 *Long future* (future): The trader who buys long silver futures contracts deposits original or initial margin (say 10 per cent of the contract value) and thereafter, if the silver price declines, may be called upon to deposit additional variation margin if the price drops. Any time the holder of long silver futures wants to buffer or hedge his downside exposure, back months may be sold short. Thus if the trader were long May 1988 silver and was worried that between January and April 1988 there might be a price relapse, this could be hedged by selling July or December silver, etc. But during the term of the hedge, if the silver prices rises instead of drops, the trader, of course, is locked in since the front month involving the long position (May) will appreciate in a rising market but the short back month (July or December) will concomitantly deteriorate during a price rise. Moreover, since this type of hedge results in a spread position, should the spread behave adversely to the market

entry points, the hedger may be called upon to deposit additional cash margins.

4   *Long future* (option): To prevent being locked in when desiring to hedge long silver futures positions, the trader would purchase protective puts. If the silver price drops, the loss in the futures would be offset by the gain in value of the positioned puts. If the price of silver rises, on the other hand, the hedger, whose downward risk is protected by the put, has his cake and eats it, since the rising market will increase the equity of the long future. Thus while the most that can be lost in the put-protected position is the cost of the put, the hedger is not locked in and therefore free to enjoy the unexpected market price rise. The disadvantage of purchasing the put for protection in this instance as compared to protection described above to the long future by going short a back month is simply that a premium had to be paid for the put. This, of course, adds to the cost of the hedging programme. But if the hedger looks at the cost of the option as down-market insurance that keeps the door open in up markets, the cost of the protective option may be well worth the expense.

5   *Long call* (future): By going short a future, the hedger who holds a silver call has protected any intrinsic value in the option. That value being the strike price of the call deducted per ounce from the market entry point of the short. Thus if a trader were long a March $7 COMEX silver call, and the COMEX March future traded at $7.60, by going short the future at that level, the hedger would nail down 60 cents an ounce ($3,000) recovery. But whilst the short future protected the paper value of the option, the holder is locked in to that precise 60-cent point. If silver then rises to say $8, the $2,000 improvement in the long call is marred by the $2,000 upward erosion of the short future.

6   *Long call* (option): Unlike the owner of the long call above who decides to lock in or nail down appreciation in the option via going short the involved future, this hedger simply purchases a put. Now the appreciation in the long call has been protected (less the cost of the put, of course) and if the silver market rises, the owner of the call protected by a put can enjoy the continued appreciation in the simulated long position represented by the call. The disadvantage of this strategy centres upon the cost of buying the protective put. But if the market takes off on the upside, shifting risk without being locked in may justify the costs.

7   *Long put* (future): If purchase of a put by a speculator or trader is held to be similar to a short sale – without the upside risk, then a successful put position, where the holder finds intrinsic value in the

option because of a down market, can be nailed down through going long the silver future (or even going long physical silver). Yet any silver price decline during the time the long put is hedged by the future or physical cannot benefit the risk-taker, who is now locked in; because if the silver price falls, the value of the long future and/or physical will also deteriorate, offsetting appreciation in the successful put. Understandably if the market rises, the long put may deteriorate or even die worthless, but the long silver or silver future will, of course, greatly appreciate.

8   *Long put* (option): Instead of being locked in against further downside appreciation by going long the future or the physical, a knowledgeable hedger might simply buy a silver call. In this strategy, if the silver price drops sharply, the put will become quite valuable. And whilst the cost of the call may be lost in part or in toto, the put holder had had the benefit of 'insurance'. If the market rises, the hedge medium, the call, will become very valuable while the long put may become worthless. The trader sitting with a valuable long put and realising that no market goes straight up or down might find it beneficial to nail down the intrinsic value in the put by purchasing a lower than strike protective call.

9   *Future inventory* (future): In this application of hedging, a silver user may confront the need to purchase silver in the cash market for future delivery as inventory. In order to assure an approximate delivery price at the time the metal might be needed, the user can go long silver futures. If the silver price rises during the interval, any cash price rise in the physicals market will be reflected approximately in the futures market. But this manoeuvre locks in the silver user and does not permit him to take advantage of a drop in the silver price, because if the price indeed drops, the loss in the futures position wil assuredly offset any benefits from decline in the cash market price. Moreover, while the long silver futures are in portfolio during a market price drop, the hedger could be called upon to deposit additional cash for maintenance (some call it variation) margin.

10   *Future inventory* (option): If the silver user, who desires protection against a possible silver price rise purchases calls instead of going long futures, leverage contracts or forward contracts, resorts to buying calls in the silver physicals or futures markets, the door is left open possibly to profit from the hedge. For example after the calls are purchased the silver price drops and by the time the silver is required, it can be bought cheaply in the cash market. If the silver price rises, as originally envisaged when the calls were bought as a user-hedge, then the calls can be exercised, or resold, and the

money gained will offset approximately the higher price the hedger is compelled to pay for his silver needs in the cash market.

11 *Short physical* (future): A bullion source that may be short physical silver to be delivered during a specific month or by a specified date can hedge successfully by buying silver futures. If the silver price rises, the equity gain in the long silver futures nullifies the increased cost in the cash market. But at the same time the hedger is locked in because any appreciation in the short physical situation is wiped out by the decline in equity in the long futures.

12 *Short physical* (option): A bullion source that may be short physical silver can hedge without being locked in by purchasing silver calls. If the market rises, the short-seller is protected by the calls since they can be exercised, and through an EFP (exchange for physicals) the actual silver can be delivered. But if the silver price plummets, the short-seller's calls will die and the short position will benefit, of course, by the market drop in the silver price.

13 *Short future* (future): Here the hedger can protect against adverse upside price movements by going long silver futures in the back or farther out months. But the position thereafter is locked in since a market drop will benefit the short future but be adverse to the long back month future. Since this type of hedge results in a spread position, the hedger may be called upon for additional cash margin if the spread becomes adverse to its market entry points.

14 *Short future* (option): Should the hedger who is short silver futures desire protection that permits possible profits, then calls on silver are purchased. In this case the short position is protected against possible market rise. But if the silver price drops as envisaged by the hedger, then the calls will expire but the short position equity will have greatly improved, possibly resulting in protected profits, depending upon, of course, the cost of the protective calls.

15 *Short call* (future): A risk-taker desirous of earning part or all of silver call premiums can sell calls short covered or naked. If desirous of protecting the short call from future price rises, the seller can shift upside risk by going long silver futures or physicals. But if the silver price drops, the cushion represented by the premiums from the calls sold may not be sufficient enough to cover the possible losses on the silver future or physical position. So the hedged, or covered, call seller is really protected against a silver price rise and not a price drop.

16 *Short call* (option): A risk-taker interested in attempting to earn premiums by writing or selling silver calls can hedge his upside risks by buying silver calls. For example, assuming a seller had sold $7 March 1988 silver calls (naked, or without protection) when silver

stood at $6.95 an ounce, the cost of $6.75 calls in the marketplace shortly after taking the initial risk of selling the $7 call were substantially cheaper because the silver had dropped below $6.50. Now if the hedger who was short the $7 calls went into the market and purchased $6.75 calls, the trader not only was assured of a profit if the market moved up, there would also have been a built-in profit if the market continued down. But the profit, of course, would have been limited to the differential between what the trader received for the $7 call and what was paid for the $6.75 call. Of course if the seller were naked and the silver market rose instead of declined, purchase of protective calls would have stopped out loss on the naked positions – with any loss limited to the cost of the premiums paid for the protection as compared with the premiums received for taking the initial risk. But unlike the protection that could have been generated as in number 15 above with long futures, the seller who buys protective calls is not subjected to further market loss above the cost of the calls if the silver price drops.

17 *Short put* (future): A seller of a put can be either naked or covered. If naked the seller's account will be charged with additional margin if the silver price declines: credited to the extent of the put premiums if it rises. The seller can hedge his risk, of course, by going short the involved silver future. Now he is considered covered and if the silver price drops the deterioration in his short put position is protected by the appreciation in the short future position, no matter how far down silver goes. But if silver rises instead of drops in price the protective short futures are only cushioned to the extent of the premiums received – and it is conceivable that in rising markets, the covered put seller can generate losses instead of profits. Moreover, if the short future is kept in position to protect the short put whilst the silver market soars, the seller may be compelled to put up more cash for margin by his broker.

18 *Short put* (option): A put seller who is naked can also be hedged through purchase of protective puts. Here should silver drop and the short put position deteriorate, the protective puts will appreciate. But if the market should rise the invasion of the risk-taker's capital is limited to the cost of the protective puts. For example, assume the risk-taker sells May 1988 COMEX silver puts (naked, or without protection) at $6.50, when COMEX May silver is at $6.75. Should July silver subsequently rise to $7.75, a $6.75 July silver put would be trading at a substantially lower premium than that received for the sale of the May $6.75 puts, when the COMEX May contract stood at $7. Purchase of the July $6.75 puts for protection would hedge the naked seller effectively against a

declining market; and assure profits no matter which way the market goes if the July puts cost less than the May puts. But those profits would be limited – until the May expirations – to the price differential between the premiums of the puts sold and those purchased. Thereafter – if the July puts have not been exercised – the seller has a bit of protection if desiring to sell silver puts for the July month.

19 *Future sale inventory* (future): A bullion source (a mine or other participant) wants to presell silver that will come out of the ground or the refinery at some future date. To assure a market price that would make the predetermined sale profitable, the hedger can resort to selling silver futures on an exchange for the delivery months anticipated. In this case, a floor price has been set for the forthcoming silver whether the market goes up or down. If the silver market rises, the loss on the short futures will be offset by the increased price of silver in the cash market. If the silver price drops the loss in the cash market by the hedger will be offset approximately by the profits from the short futures. But in this case, of course, the hedger is locked in during the term of the protection achieved with futures.

20 *Future sale inventory* (option): If the bullion source desires protection during a set time period and decides to hedge by purchasing puts instead of, as in number 19 above, going short silver futures, the funds expended for the put purchases are the most at risk. The floor price is the put strike less the cost of the put. But the hedger is free to sell his silver in the cash market for much higher prices – if the silver market rises. In other words, by hedging with put purchases, the mine or bullion source has downside price protection plus the opportunity possibly for upside profits.

HEDGING CONSIDERATIONS AND CONCEPTS

Previously there have been listed some of the major hedging strategies available to those who own silver, who intend to buy or to sell silver in the future, who are long and/or short silver futures and options, etc. But it wouldn't be fair to call a halt here to this subject wihtout expanding on the concepts and considerations applicable to the subject of silver hedging.

Hedging theory

A silver hedger is basically interested in shifting the price risk involved in conducting his business, financing, or speculating in silver operations.

In essence, therefore, protecting or locking in a risk position is the paramount concept in utilising silver hedging strategies. Because hedging has its costs, as well as benefits the primary questions a silver hedger has to answer are: (a) Is there a need for the contemplated hedge? (b) What factors are involved in structuring the hedge? (c) How long should the hedge be in effect? (d) What strategies for hedging should be used? and (e) How costly will the contemplated price protection be?

Theoretically then, a hedger, one would think, should be content to act positively to (a) protect capital assets (as in the case of a bullion source that owns or expects to create silver); (b) protect contractual risks (as in the case of fabricators at some future date; or speculators who may be compelled to receive or deliver silver or silver futures at some future date); and (c) be aware of all costs involved in the various hedging strategies selected.

But as is often the case in other areas of risk subject to price change, theory and practice often travel diverse roads. Hedgers who should use protection decide to speculate; and speculators decide to hedge when they should be taking risks.

Hedging practice

Whether the potential hedger is a silver producer, user, service source, including financing, or speculator, the first thing to accomplish once the need for protection is decided upon, is to construct the hedge.

Structuring the hedge is perhaps one of the most important aspects of the hedge process in that the price-protecting elements have to be assembled to suit the quantity of silver in physical or paper form that has to be hedged. Once the hedge media have been selected – and the amount of silver to be hedged fixed – the term of the hedge has to be determined. In this regard, the hedger decides for how long and for how much silver the protective measures should be installed. Then the costs of the hedging strategies selected (trading commissions; interest rates, or whatever) should be carefully examined and included in the price targets that are to be protected. Once all this has been accomplished; and the hedge is installed it now has to be managed.

Managing the hedge

Managing the hedge involves both discipline and flexibility. If the policy of the hedger is simply to install a hedge and leave it on until the protected silver arrives or is delivered, then the hedge is a rigid one and must be kept unchanged. If the hedger has a flexible approach, the protection may be added to or subtracted, held longer than the anticipated delivery dates or lifted before they arrive, etc. Since no two silver producers, users or speculators operate precisely in the same manner, the chances are that the silver hedging programme will also vary. But in every case, the hedge must make sense or else it has to be altered or done away with. So despite murmurs from professionals to the contrary, flexibility, in the author's opinion, is as important in managing the hedge as its original structuring.

The decisions by the hedge managers, of course, may arise often as not from market conditions. And in some cases the hedge instruments might either not be readily available or might be too expensive to purchase.

When silver becomes volatile either upward or downward in price, the premiums of silver options escalate, causing them to be far more expensive than during periods of silver quietude. (Of course, in a rising market the call premiums increase and in a falling market the put premiums increase.) To offset these costs, it might make sense for the hedger to use both options and futures as the hedging instruments via conversions and reverse conversions. In any event, if the hedge is properly structured – unless market conditions change abruptly – a minimum of management is needed. But if the hedge has not been properly structured, managing it is necessary.

For example, the author was once sent to Lima, Peru, in mid-1980 to help educate the Peruvians how to hedge their silver production. As some readers may already know, in December 1979 the Peruvian government silver marketing agency (Minero Peru Commercial or MINPECO) had lost $80 million in silver short positions when they were unable to deliver physical silver of exchange grade in conforming to outstanding short silver contracts. The loss came because they were short at about $18 an ounce and were bought in by their brokers at much higher levels. But the Peruvian hedge was structured in such a way that, with an estimated production of about 3 million silver ounces in December, they were short about six times that amount. The Peruvians were 'over-hedged'.

It seems that at that time most of the Peruvian miners delivered concentrate (ore containing silver and other metals) to MINPECO who paid the miners promptly for the metal in the concentrates. Then the concentrates were shipped to Mexico, where after six months or so the concentrated ore became refined silver. Since MINPECO didn't have the funds to pay the miners at the time the concentrates were delivered, they borrowed silver from the National Bank of Peru, sold the silver to get cash, and then replaced the silver with the refined silver from Mexico. But in the meantime – and to protect themselves from another price rise – MINPECO at the time it borrowed silver from its bank also went long silver futures on COMEX to hedge against a possible price rise.

The obvious error in this hedging strategy involved the possibility of silver declining in price until the Peruvian silver in Mexico came down to Lima. If the silver had risen in price, the appreciation in the long silver futures would offset the rise in price of the refined silver that had to be returned to the National Bank at the price it was loaned to MINPECO. But if silver declined in price MINPECO could lose in *two* ways: (a) they would have advanced the miners too high a price for the silver represented by the concentrates; and (b) they would have suffered a loss in the futures on COMEX held to 'insure' that they were able to return the silver to the bank at the original price of borrowing.

Bullion firms employ several methods of hedging. For example a bullion source that maintains silver inventory generally resorts to short silver futures for hedging purposes. Whenever bullion in the cash market is sold from the inventory, the number of short futures is contracted to conform to their hedging programme. Whenever more bullion is added to inventory more exchange futures are sold short. In this manner, the bullion source is at all times without risk. If the market rises and it loses on the short futures it liquidates when making a cash bullion sale, the higher the price in the cash market eases the pain of the futures market loss. If the silver price has declined and the bullion source is called upon to supply silver to the cash market, then the profits on the short futures will offset the loss in the cash silver sale. What is being related here is that the bullion source doesn't care if the silver price goes up or down. It cannot afford to take continuous risks since most of its bullion is pledged in the first place. So that silver, hedged by the short futures, is silver with the risk transferred to whoever bought the long futures contracts. And when the short futures contracts used for the bullion hedge are liquidated, the risk involved in the physical silver then shifts to the new owner of the cash silver – with the bullion source winding up with a 'profit in pennies' above their hedging costs.

6

SILVER TRADING MECHANICS

Silver trading is broadly divided into three parts:

1 The bullion market.
2 The paper futures market, which also includes leverage contracts and their equivalent called 'forwards'.
3 The silver options markets, which include options on silver futures, dealer and exchange-traded options on physicals; and commercial trade options.

In order to pose the mechanics of buying and selling in these various trading media, this chapter is arbitrarily divided into the foregoing major topics. It begins with trading mechanics in the silver bullion market.

SILVER BULLION TRADING MECHANICS

In Chapter 1 the forms of silver bullion were described – and these included not only the standard 1,000-ounce silver bars, but also smaller bars, bullion coins, and objects formed from silver of various grades. But the serious silver trader will probably seek profits from dealing in silver bars deliverable into organised markets such as the various silver futures exchanges, the LME and the London silver market. Silver stored in exchange-approved warehouses is fully described as to weight and purity on negotiable warehouse receipts (also known as 'warrants').

Assuming further that the trader in silver bullion intends to trade with warehouse receipts, those receipts should be kept and stored in a safe depository. In addition, since the trader may have to resort to paper silver markets either for hedging or for delivery, the receipts should be kept in an account at the brokerage firm which will be 'clearing' the trader's business. The meanings of 'clearing' in this sense on behalf of the trader are: (a) execution of buy and/or sell orders; (b) receipt or delivery of the physical metal; and (c) receipt of payment for metal sold and delivered and/or payment of funds for metal purchased and received. Illustrative of such service sources are firms like Rudolf Wolf, an LME member with offices and agents on a global basis; or Shearson, which has global bullion trading facilities. The trader can carry a bullion account at a bank that specialises in servicing such activity, like Rhode Island Hospital Trust, Delaware Bank, Republic Bank of New York, in America; or Banks of England and on the continent such as Dresdner Bank in Frankfurt, Credit Suisse or Union Bank in Switzerland.

In the conduct of buying and selling physical silver, the trader is either subject to commissions – if the brokerage firm or bank acts as agent – or mark ups and discounts, if the bullion intermediary acts as a principal. Generally the commissions for large transactions are quite small: For small transactions they may seem quite large. In addition to commissions for agency transactions and/or mark ups/discounts, if the silver accommodator acts as principal, there are storage and insurance charges for the silver represented by the warrants or the warehouse receipts. There are also shipping handling and delivery charges whenever silver bullion is transferred from one locale to another. Since the commissions, mark up/discounts, storage insurance and delivery charges vary not only by the size of the physical transactions, but also often by their frequency; and since these fees may vary between customers using such facilities, it is prudent to first determine precisely what all the charges are before beginning to trade.

For example, an account at a bullion bank may be paying a half per cent of the annual value of silver stored in the bank vaults of an approved exchange warehouse, while another account at the same bullion bank, whose holdings are much larger than the customer being charged a half per cent may be paying only a quarter per cent.

Obviously transaction, storage and delivery charges make inroads on any profits a trader may be fortunate enough to earn trading physical silver.

One strategy open to the bullion trader that has not been discussed previously is the 'cash and carry'. In this case, the owner of silver bullion can go short in the futures market in a far-out delivery month and lock in a gain on the silver because of the contango existing in the futures market. This gain is restricted to the contango, less whatever the charges to deliver the bullion against the short future will entail. Since the contango is approximately the going REPO rate, the bullion holder who resorts to this strategy has no downside risk, no upside profit chance over and above the differential between the sales price in the futures month and the market entry price to purchase the silver bullion. Some traders use the futures market to create the bullion involved in the cash and carry. For example, the investor goes long a March 1988 COMEX silver future and simultaneously goes short the July delivery of the same year. When the March future becomes the spot or cash month, the investor takes delivery of the actual bullion via the warehouse receipt, pays for the bullion, and holds it until the first delivery date of the July future, which is the last business day in June, and tenders the bullion to the risk-taker who happens to still be open long in the July future.

To come out ahead in such a transaction, the investor, who has held the bullion at no risk during the interim, must be able to presell the bullion via the July future at a diffential greater than the loss of money use entailed by the funds locked up in the physical silver, plus whatever costs the transactions will entail. Those readers who may want to apply mathematics to this situation may use the following formula:

$$R = \left(\frac{(P_2 - P_1) - c}{P_1} \right) \left(\frac{360}{t} \right)$$

In the above formula:

R = Implied annual return
P_2 = Price of short far silver future
P_1 = Price of silver bullion or near future
c = Costs per ounce storage and insurance for the carry term
t = time in the number of days between the bullion and the short future or between the near and the far silver futures.

Source: The Metals Consultancy

Silver bullion orders

Unless circumstances are beyond the trader's control, such as when bullion is bought because of delivery default, or because it is tendered to a long future during the delivery month, a long that is still open and not offset, the orders to buy or sell should be at specific prices – and not at market price.

The bullion buyer, like a securities buyer who must have 'action' of an immediate nature, can always enter market orders to buy or sell silver in the physical market, just as the trader can in the paper silver market, if desired. Also a specific quantity should be appended to any order to buy or to sell silver bullion. Moreover, the seller should be aware of the location where the solid silver is to be delivered; and in the same way the buyer should be aware of where the purchased bullion is stored.

For example, if an owner of New York stored silver sold into the London market on a cash basis, that silver would have to be delivered 'loco London' the following day. So before effecting such a sale, the seller in New York would have to arrange a location swap through a bullion source, which might entail a small expense. Conversely silver bought in London could readily be swapped – in normal markets – for silver in New York, etc.

As has already been noted, owners of bona fide silver bullion warehouse receipts or warrants can lever them by borrowing varying percentages of the capital involved in the silver. Such silver loans, usually from a bullion banking source, may vary from 50 to 90 per cent depending on the creditworthiness of the borrower and the willingness of the lending source to assume market risks. In this connection, the chances are that silver hocked for 90 per cent of its market value would be protected from downside ravages by some sort of hedge.

Since the charges for bullion-related services of all kinds, as mentioned vary, it is prudent to predetermine every kind of charge in every kind of situation the silver trader in bullion expects to encounter.

PAPER SILVER TRADING MECHANICS

The world of paper silver involves (a) futures, leverage and forward contracts; (b) options on futures and physicals; and (c) certificates. Since silver certificates are evidence of bullion stored at a safe facility, they may be disposed of as retail 'warehouse certificates or warrants'. Since these certificates are in effect being vended retail by a wholesale source it follows that they are as safe and as reliable as the sources that issue them.

Since leverage contracts and forward arrangements are between the customer and the bullion source, a reliable leveraging source should be chosen. Unlike leverage and forward contracts, which are created between customer and dealer, or dealer-agent, exchange-traded futures and options on physicals provide the risk-taker with contracts guaranteed by a clearing house. So that if the exchange member behind the contracts is unable to fulfil the contracts, the clearing house will see to fulfilment.

In this connection, it is suggested that purchasers and sellers of forward and leverage contracts deal only with firms authorised by the CFTC to deal with the retail public; and that commercial firms (silver mines and silver users) who seek hedging manoeuvres deal only with recognised bullion sources who are members of organised markets.

Exchange-traded silver futures

There are basically only two strategies shouted via public outcry in the silver trading pits, long buy contracts and short sell contracts. Spreads (simultaneous buy and sell of two differing delivery silver futures months) are done with specialists out of the ring called spread-makers, and the first report from the floor on such trades is the differential between the months. The market entry price for each side of the spread can be set at the highs or the lows of the price during that session. See page 44 for more information about spreads. Also performed out of the pits are EFP transactions. These 'exchange for physicals' permit the holder of a long futures contract that has not matured to the cash month to exchange the contract for actual delivery of the silver. In reverse manner, holders of silver bullion of exchange grade in exchange warehouses can swap their bullion positions in physicals for long positions in futures, if desired.

But since the silver futures price is beamed all over the world during trading sessions and carried to the ends of the earth over at least seven differing information services, price discovery of silver for delivery of say up to eighteen months at least is readily evident to screen watchers of videos that carry those information services.

Silver futures orders

Buy and sell orders originated at a broker for execution on an organised exchange trading silver futures must bear the words 'buy' or 'sell'; the delivery month desired to be bought or sold; the number of contracts to be bought or sold; the name and account number of the person or company for whom the order is being entered; and the conditions attendant to the order (whether it is at a specific price limit, at market, etc.). Of course, the account number of the service person who is to be credited with commission for the order, if and when it is executed, is also on the buy/sell ticket. Also, when the ticket is written by the service person it is time-stamped and given to an order clerk for transmission to the trading floor. Upon receipt of the fill (report of the trade) the ticket is again time-stamped. But life for the people who have to fulfil customer's wishes when it comes to silver orders would be simple if the orders were just buy and/or sell. However, there are conditions attendant on each buy or sell order that make life complicated for those who serve. In order to understand this, here are the kinds of silver orders that may be entered to buy or sell specific silver futures, for example on COMEX.

1 *Day order*: All orders to buy or sell silver placed through COMEX exchange members are orders which if not filled during the trading session automatically die. If the account specifies GTC (good till cancelled) a new ticket must be sent to the pit each day until the order is filled or cancelled by the customer. Some firms therefore will take only day orders and no GTC orders.

2 *GTC order*: These are orders to buy or sell silver futures that are 'good till cancelled' by the customer. But because of conditions stated

above under day order, some firms will only accept GTW orders (good the week). Normally a GTC order, if accepted by the servicing firm, will have to be renewed by the customer every month in order to remain alive. This kind of order, therefore, is GTM (good the month).

3 *Market order*: This condition to a buy or sell order means the best prevailing silver price at the time the order is worked in the pits.

4 *Limit order*: In this type of order to buy or sell the order to buy is generally below the going market; and the order to sell, above it. But if the market, in the case of the limit-buy order, declines to that limit it should be executed; and in the case of the limit-sell order if the market rises to the specified limit it should go off. The problem is that if the price does not go past the limit but reverses the order may not be executed even though the future did trade at the specified limits. That is why traders who want immediate action at or about specific price levels use buy-stops or sell-stops, explained below.

5 *Stop order* (also known as stop loss orders): orders to buy or to sell silver futures that bear a price limit and the word 'stop' automatically becomes market orders if the specified limit is reached. If the limit is not reached the order will not be executed. For example a holder of long March COMEX silver futures with a market entry price of $6.50 sees the market rally to $7.00. He may enter a sell-stop at $6.75 so that if the market suddenly reacts downward his position might be liquidated. In practice, should the silver price drop to $6.75 chances are the stop, which becomes market at that point will be triggered, but the execution price may be below the specified $6.75 limit level.

Conversely, a short in March COMEX silver at $7 may see silver drop to $6.75 and enter an order below the market to buy silver say at $6.50 stop. If silver does dip to that level while the order is in effect, it will become market and be executed. But again the buy limit of $6.50 might turn out to be a higher price when the order is filled. Since the holder of a long silver future is interested primarily in stop-loss during declining markets and the holder of a short future is interested in stop-loss in a rising market, the stop-loss sell order will always be below the market and the stop-loss buy order always above the market.

6 *Miscellaneous orders*: Among the many other types of orders, which may or may not be acceptable at the firms where the trade conducts business, are miscellaneous orders such as: (a) *fill or kill*, meaning all or none; (b) *stop-limit*, meaning the order is activated when the price reaches the stop but cannot be filled beyond a specified price; (c) *market-if-touched*, meaning just like a limit order but goes off at the market if the limit is reached; (d) *contingent*, meaning a market order

in one future if the market is reached in the silver future of a differing delivery; (e) *OCO* (*one cancels the other*), meaning there are two orders at differing prices – and perhaps differing delivery months – but if one order is filled the other is automatically cancelled; (f) *market at close*, meaning some price within the closing range of a silver future; and (g) *market at open*, meaning some price within the opening range of the specified future. So before conducting any business at any service firm determine precisely what orders the firm will accept to buy or sell silver futures on the various exchanges, since the chances are that many of the above miscellaneous orders will not be acceptable.

7 *Spread orders*: If the trader wants to spread silver futures, one silver future month is bought and one is simultaneously sold. The way the order is put in is to specify which month should be bought and which sold – with how much of a differential. For example, buy the March and sell the May with 8 cents premium of May over March, etc.

Silver futures margins

Once the kind of orders to buy or sell futures have been determined, the next important item for traders is to consider the 'house' requirements for margins (good faith deposits) prevalent at the firm where business is to be conducted. In this regard, the requirements may differ somewhat from the exchange minimum margin requirements, depending on the creditworthiness of the customer. So that at one firm – with exchange silver future initial or original margins per contract at $2,500, house requirements might be $5,000 for speculators of one kind and say $4,000 for others. Exchange hedger original margins might be $1,500, but the house might require $2,000, etc.

In addition, maintenence or variation margin levels may differ from exchange requirements. Understandably since margins are good faith deposits that guarantee the soundness of the clearing member and the involved clearing house, it may be that both original margin requirements and maintenance margins are pegged a little higher than exchange minimums.

At most firms who are members of exchanges where silver futures are actively traded such as COMEX and CBOT, T-bills are acceptable as original margin. But variation or maintenance margin must be supplied or received daily to and from the exchange clearing house by the clearing member for the trader's account in the form of cash.

For example, a trader deposits $50,000 to open an account to trade in silver futures and goes long two May 1988 COMEX silver futures at $7 market entry price. The trader's service firm will put the $50,000 into

T-bills (three-months or six-months maturities as desired). Then the service firm will deposit T-bills at the clearing house to satisfy original (initial) margin requirements. The next day the closing price of May silver is $7.20. The clearing house will credit the service firm on behalf of the trader with the 20 cents per ounce market appreciation in equity or $2,000 (20 cents x 10,000 ounces in the two contracts). The trader can *use* or *withdraw* that $2,000 for any purpose, without paying any interest. If the next day silver continues its rise and gains another 20 cents an ounce, the account will be credited (in cash) with another $2,000.

Conversely, if the silver price from point of entry at $7 dropped 40 cents to $6.60, the service firm would have to send maintenance margin of $4,000 in cash (certified cheque) to the clearing house and the account would be called upon for additional funds – if it were the policy of the service firm to have the accounts 'mark-to-the-market' for margin purposes. Although it is wise, of course, to ascertain in advance the margin policy of the firm where silver futures trading is to be conducted, the trader must realise that those conditions are subject to immediate change – and retroactive (that is affecting positions already in the account) – at the behest of the servicing firm.

Options on silver futures

There are two kinds of options on silver futures: 1. Calls, giving the holder the right to have a long silver future positioned in the holder's account – with a concomitant short silver future at the call-strike automatically positioned in the seller's or writer's account. 2. Puts, providing the holder with the right to sell a silver future at the strike of the puts – with a concomitant long silver future position delivered to the put-seller's account at the strike of the puts. Combinations of these options on silver futures make up the various spreads of options on silver futures.

Since the call and put buyers pay a premium to buy the silver call or put from the seller, who receives the premium, the exercise of the option is at the 'call' or choice of the holder. In both cases, puts and calls, the item being optioned is – if on COMEX – 5,000-ounce silver futures: And if on CBOT, 1,000-ounce silver futures. Since the exercise privilege exists at the behest of the holder from time of purchase till a specified time on the expiration date, buyers of silver puts and calls should predetermine precisely until what time their service firm will act to exercise existing options owned by the trader on the last date of life.

All options on silver futures have uniform expiration dates: the second Friday of the month preceding the contract month of the option.

Thus the buyer of a May 1988 COMEX $7 silver call must know that the call has to be exercised or die by a certain time on the second Friday in April. The buyer of a July $6.75 COMEX silver put has to know that the option expires on the second Friday in June, etc. This, of course, is necessary because these are options on futures, not physicals, and the holders of successful calls, for example, can position the silver futures involved via exercise, hold the futures into the delivery or spot month, and accept the physical silver allegedly under the future when tendered. The following illustrates the relative positions of buyers and sellers of options on silver futures:

Option position	Simulated future	Open risk	P/L
(a) Long silver call	Long silver future	Option cost	Profits
(b) Long silver put	Short silver future	Option cost	Profits
(c) Short silver call	Short silver future	Unlimited	Loss
(d) Short silver put	Long silver future	Unlimited	Loss

Source: The Metals Consultancy

Addressing the above items one at a time:

(a) *Long silver call*: The holder (buyer) of a call on a silver future may be considered in the light of a speculator holding a long silver future. If the price rises the call becomes more valuable. If the price drops, the call loses value. But the most the call-buyer can ever lose is the cost of the involved option. Thus his total open risk, as indicated above, is confined to the cost of the call – and his profits are unlimited on the upside if the silver price keeps risking. But if the price collapses, there is never a margin call.

(b) *Long silver put*: The holder (buyer) of a put on a silver future may be considered the same as a speculator who is short a silver future – without upside risk other than the cost of the put. Profits may be held to be unlimited if the silver price keeps dropping. And should the silver price rise instead of fall there is never a margin call.

(c) *Short silver call*: The seller of a call on a silver future is similar to a short in a silver future. If the seller of the call does not have the physical or is not long a silver future to be covered, but is instead naked, any possible profit – if silver declines during the life of the call – is restricted to the amount of the premium received (less transaction costs). But if the silver price rises, the seller of the short call is exposed to unlimited risks, including demands for additional cash margins.

(d) *Short silver put*: The risk-taker who sells silver future puts may be likened to a trader who goes long silver futures. Except that any profit – if the silver price rises – is limited to the premiums received for the puts (less transaction charges); and any price decline may trigger demands for more margin if the trader has sold the puts naked. Of course, the trader can limit risk on the downside by going short the future as a cover. But if the silver market should thereafter rise, the trader could find himself being asked for margin. Thus as in the converse case of selling calls, the seller has limited chance for gain and unlimited chances for loss.

Option selling exceptions

There are two special cases of exception for option sellers. These are the possibility of preselling silver above the actual market; or attempting to buy it below the actual market.

If a trader owns physical silver and wants to try to presell it above the actual physical market at the time of trading, he can sell a call on a silver future. If the price rises and the call is exercised, the owner of the physical silver can offset his risk by liquidating the short silver position in his futures account assigned by the clearing house and simultaneously selling his silver in the cash market. The ensuing profit should return a price higher than the going silver market at the time of selling the call.

If the trader wants to try to buy silver under the market at the time of trading, the strategy would be to sell a naked put. If the market declines and the put is exercised, the trader has purchased the ensuing silver position at lower than the price prevailing at time of undertaking the risk, by virtue of the premium received for the sale of the put.

Understandably, in the case of the call seller who is trying to presell his silver above market at the time of the trade, should the silver price drop, the call might die and the seller would earn the premium involved (less the transaction charges, of course) but might not have been able to dispose of the silver at a favourable price. And in the case of the put-seller, if the silver price rose and the put died, the trader would, of course, earn the premium involved but would not receive the desired silver position. So it should be remembered that the only way a trader can possibly presell silver above the market at time of a trade is to sell calls; and the only way a trader can try to position silver under the market is to sell puts against cash.

Options on futures orders

Options on silver futures are involved with the same kind of orders as applicable to the futures themselves: i.e. limit, market, etc. The difference lies in orders involving options on silver futures spreads. In this case one or more options are bought and simultaneously sold. For horizontal or vertical spreads there will be a net credit or a net debit. The same goes for butterflies or other complicated manoeuvres. So whenever a spread order for options on silver futures is considered it should not contain specific buy and sell prices for the involved options, but rather specific net credit or debit parameters.

Other exchange-traded silver options

The EOE, European Options Exchange, trades options on physical silver in contracts covering 250 ounces per contract. These are traded in Amsterdam, Montreal, and Singapore, for example, but the bulk of silver option trading is confined to the activities on COMEX and CBOT in the form of options on silver futures. The EOE options evidently were envisaged for small speculators on the one hand and for option holders who actually wanted to take delivery on the silver if the calls became successful. Since these options are traded European Style (exercise on last day only) the premiums are less than the premiums for exchange-traded options on silver futures, which can be exercised at any time during life by the holders.

Dealer options on physical silver

At the time of writing several firms in the US, such as MONEX, are permitted by the CFTC to retail options on physical silver. These options are generally bought from the dealer and sold back to him or exercised by the holder. The dealer, of course, operates with a spread, that is he markets the physical silver options with a mark up and buys them back with a discount. In this regard, Mocatta Metals, back in the days before the CFTC went into business pioneered the marketing of Mocatta silver options (at that time in 10,000-ounce contracts) through selected dealers, including some stock exchange members. When the dealer-option-format supervised by the CFTC arose after 1978, the Mocatta-type dealer puts and calls of 1,000-ounce and less units, became quite popular. But before buying Mocatta silver calls, or MONEX silver calls, or calls from any other source authorised by the CFTC to be sold to the retail public, all the details of pricing on purchase and pricing on resale should be determined, including precisely what the expiration dates of those options turn out to be.

Trade options on physical silver

Trade puts and calls concern options bought and sold by commercial producers and users primarily for hedging purposes. Creation of these options in the main involves providing either a floor price for the producer for a definite time period or a ceiling price for the user during specified terms. They are generally made, for example, between mining firms like Coeur d'Alene Corporation and Engelhard; between Mocatta and Maytag, a company that buys silver for washing machine contacts, etc. On rare occasions in the past, when the quantity involved was rather large options were done by these bullion sources with large private speculators. But since the CFTC took over supervision of silver options on physicals traded to the public the author believes that such activity by wholesale sources with private speculators has ended.

Leverage contracts and forwards

Initially, leverage contracts or 'forwards' were created to service the actual needs of silver producers and users. Thus when Sunshine Mining Company was actively mining silver, it sold its output to Engelhard. But Sunshine some years ago decided to provide silver bullion in convenient 1-ounce, 10-ounce and 100-ounce forms to the general public. To do this on a practical basis Sunshine had to buy silver blanks or strips from Engelhard in order to produce the coin-like medallions or wafers to be marketed. As a result Sunshine had to make forward arrangements with Engelhard to make sure there was a ceiling price on the silver strips Sunshine would require to punch out the coins and wafers.

In the MONEX type of leverage contract the customer who wants to own physical silver in this form deposits say 25 per cent of the value of the contract and carries the position forward as long as desired. Interestingly, unlike a silver futures contract which has to be 'rolled forward' when the cash month arrives along with a resultant loss from the contango, the leverage contract can continue into the next century, if the holder desires. In any event, in order to compare fairly what it would cost to carry a paper position long in COMEX futures for say a year, the trader should get all the details pertaining to leverage contracts and thus be armed with the intelligence needed to make the comparison.

For example, if in November 1987 a trader wanted to go long March 1988 futures on COMEX and then when February came decided he wanted to keep the position but roll it forward to July 1988, the trader would have to liquidate the March longs and go long the July. This would result, of course, in commissions. Then when June came if the trader wanted to extend the silver position by rolling it to December, more commissions would arise, etc. In addition to the commissions, the point of market entry is another consideration. If there were a 12-cent premium in the market price of March 1988 silver over December 1987, when the trader would go to roll forward the futures position to July 1988 in February 1988 the contango may have spread to 14 cents, etc.

Participation in the volatile world of silver trading requires self-education in the mechanics of ordering long or short positions in any – and perhaps all – of the available silver markets. The large trader will, of course, maintain accounts at one or more service firms. And may even maintain accounts at bullion financing sources. Since the margin requirements for buying and selling the diverse media in the various markets may vary from time to time because of the volatility in the silver price, it makes sense to never be over-extended; always to have a cash reserve, and to have sources from which to achieve protection when needed. The Talmud asks 'Who is wise?'; and the answer is, 'He who learns'. Silver traders would be very wise to learn all they can about the markets they intend to take risks before they participate – and not after.

7

SILVER FUNDAMENTAL RESEARCH

In olden – and perhaps more golden – times both silver and gold were considered the only kind of money anyone could trust. Central banks of governments generally stockpiled both precious metals as reserves behind the paper money in circulation. But silver's role as money in circulation in the United States came mainly to an abrupt end in 1964 – and when in 1968 the US Treasury redeemed outstanding silver certificates in exchange for Federal Reserve notes that had no promises behind them, but merely claimed to be 'legal tender for all debts public and private', one of silver's leading roles since Biblical times seemed headed for extinction.

In recent times, silver has had a bit of monetary resurgence with some 70-odd governments who minted the metal in coin form – mainly for collectors – in order for the governments to profit on the differential between what the silver in the coins amounted to costwise and the currency garnered when sold to the collector-minded public. In the United States in 1986, for example, the Mint issued several silver collector-coins; and also offered the business strike 'silver eagle', which bears a walking Liberty on its obverse (the eagle is on the reverse of the coin). This coin, marketed through a wholesale network of approved dealers, charged a premium of $1 per coin by the Mint for the seignorage, turned out to be highly successful; and had something of an impact on one of the important silver fundamentals, demand.

During the past few years, the utilisation of hi-tech mining methods, which mostly means heap leaching precious metal ores with cyanide solutions, also has made at impact on a silver fundamental that researchers follow, namely, supply. Because silver is a cost-intensive metal, the cost of bringing the ore from the bowels of the earth in hard-rock mines varies in the various silver producing sectors of the globe. Thus the cost basis per ounce of silver in primary silver mines (where silver is the dominant metal in the untreated ore) may be as high as US$8.50 an ounce (or more) in Idaho, where miners are union members; and naturally this is far above the cost per ounce in areas like Mexico and Peru, where labour doesn't receive the kind of hourly pay and benefits afforded to Americans. That is why, for example, Hecla Mining and Sunshine Mining shut down their Idaho hard rock mines for some years because the cost of extraction of an ounce of silver was far higher than the daily average market price of the metal in the physical markets of the world. Yet during 1986 and into 1987 low cost silver from heap leaching operations in Nevada, Montana, etc. continued to be actively unearthed at profits above the actual cost.

With this brief introduction to a few of the factors involved in the silver fundamental scene, it is now proper to delineate what the major fundamental factors are; how they impact on the going silver price; how to find the silver fundamentals; and how to combine fundamental research with a technical approach in order to make intelligent silver trading decisions.

MAJOR SILVER FUNDAMENTALS

Supply

First, of course, comes the supply part of the silver fundamentals. Components of silver supply fundamentals include the following: 1 Newly mined silver. 2 Refined silver stocks. 3 Exchange stocks. 4 Industrial inventory. 5 Government and central bank stocks. 6 Recycled silver. 7 Private silver stocks, sometimes called conjectural stocks.

1   *Newly mined silver*: These are the number of troy ounces or tonnes of silver taken from the earth each year from primary silver mines and from mines where silver is a secondary metal to other precious metals or to base metals like zinc and lead. Generally, the published information available for interested researchers or investors involves silver from sources in the free world. New silver supply in socialist or planned economy countries like the USSR and China involves estimates, which can be questionable, to say the least.

2   *Refined silver stocks*: Figures for all known refiners in Australia, Canada, Mexico, Peru, South Africa, Sweden, and many other refiners in Europe and Asia, are published reguarly by the Silver Institute, in Washington, DC. The numbers include refined silver from (a) primary ores and concentrates; (b) melt-down of silver coins; (c) 'old' scrap, such as used photographic and x-ray film; and (d) 'new' scrap, such as in-plant clippings and silver waste. The Silver Institute points out: 'Production of refined silver from new scrap is 999 silver made from in-plant clippings, spillage, sweepings, etc. generated during manufacturing processes. Since it is in a

continuous cycle from new scrap, to 999 silver, to new scrap, some researchers like to see the production and disposal totals of refined silver after deducting the new scrap from both'. The *Silver Institute Letter* not only provides the refined silver production from reporting sources, but also the disposal by these refiners. In this connection, disposal includes (a) converted in-plant, meaning consumed in fabrication, etc.; and (b) number of ounces of silver shipped out, which in turn are broken down into ounces owned by the refiners and ounces created for others by the refiners. The publication, of course, then sets the disposal of the refined silver against the amount created by production during the same period and winds up with two salient numbers: (a) refiners' stocks at end of subject period; and (b) resulting change of these refiners' stocks (production minus disposal). Since silver from ore or concentrate consumes as much as six months time to become refined to 999 purity, the level of refiners stocks – and the changes in these levels – indicate 'tightness' or 'surplus' of available metal for industrial purposes.

3 *Exchange stocks*: The silver bars acceptable as to weight and purity reposing in exchange-approved warehouses professionally are known as 'exchange stocks'. Usually reported by the exchanges on a weekly basis, changes in the levels of these stocks play an important role in assessing the fundamental impact of short-sellers of futures being able to obtain access to silver in case delivery is demanded by holders of the long futures. But the ownership of exchange stocks doesn't actually mean that the shorts can get the silver if and when it is needed for delivery against futures that have matured into the spot or cash month. The levels of exchange stocks popularly watched are those reported by the LME, the CBOT, and COMEX. In recent times of so-called normal silver markets, COMEX stocks approximate 150 million troy ounces, LME and CBOT stocks about 20 million ounces each.

4 *Industrial inventory*: The largest usage of silver in industry is in photography. Manufacturers of film maintain inventory of silver, and so do other silver users. Because inventory levels vary according to interest rates, and money use by the manufacturers; and because bullion sources have innovated such strategies as actually keeping consigned silver on the premises of the user, billing the user only when silver is drawn down from the consignment, industrial levels today of silver inventory – despite its relatively low cash price to the gold price – is to say the least minimal. Of course, these inventory levels of industrial silver users would rise upward quickly if and when the silver price rose to again be aligned realistically with the going gold price. But until interest rates on money and costs of

hedging decline from current levels, the chances are the silver inventory stocked inside a manufacturing plant may very well belong to another owner.

5 *Government and central bank silver stocks*: India, where silver is controlled by the government, is one central banking storehouse of silver bullion. So are the national banks of Mexico and Peru. In the United States, the Treasury still has a small stockpile of silver, but the bulk of government silver reposes in the national stockpile. At one time after World War II there were about 3 billion silver ounces in the stockpile. Currently there are about 100 million ounces left. After the war the government minted dimes, quarters, half-dollars and dollars of 90 per cent silver, which drained a lot of silver out of the Treasury and stockpile. Then in 1968, when outstanding silver certificates were turned into the Treasury in return for their silver worth (about $1.29, or more) much more silver disappeared from government stocks. The dwindling of government silver stocks could be translated as being a bullish fundamental – with the silver price today about four times higher than it was when the government stopped putting silver into quarters. In any event, US government stocks are divided into: (a) National Strategic Stockpile silver; (b) Treasury Department silver; (c) Department of Defense silver; and (d) Other Agency silver, such as the Veterans' Administration (silver recovery from batteries, pacemakers, etc.).

6 *Recycled silver*: When in January, 1980 the silver price soared toward $50 an ounce, fevered sellers dragged silver candlesticks and other objects bearing untold millions of dollars worth of beauty and craftsmanship to depots set up by bullion sources to turn this valuable scrap into refined silver, regardless of the value of its inherent artistry. Moreover, people were bursting into these places with teeth containing silver fillings that still had blood on the roots. Some market researchers are convinced that the level of recycled silver is directly related to the direction of the silver price. So that if the price rises there will be a flood of silver scrap inundating the market and depressing it until the flood becomes a rather thin trickle.

7 *Private silver stocks*: Nobody really knows how much silver today is in private hands. According to Mocatta Metals, its sister company Mocatta Goldsmid, has been sending silver to India for four centuries without very much of the metal coming back into the market. In India silver is the bread of life for certain castes and is worn not only for ornamental and religious reasons, but also as a monetary reserve when needed. No one really knows how many millions of silver ounces are hoarded in the form of old US coins containing silver,

wafers, bars and medallions that look like silver coins. Broadly, these private silver stocks may be categorised as (a) Unreported bullion stocks; (b) Potentially available US silver coins; and (c) Other potentially available coins. Walter Frankland, Executive Director of the Silver Users Association, estimates that private silver stocks have been added to at the rate of 5 million ounces a month for years. But since it is virtually impossible to get a handle on what goes on in this area, it is really difficult, if not impossible, to come up with an accurate number. For example, we can determine how many silver dollars were minted each year going back to the nineteenth century by the US Mint. But we cannot determine accurately how many of these dollars were melted down and reformed into American Indian silver rings, bracelets and neckpieces, including those beautiful bolos shaped like flying eagles. Unlike the surplus each year of gold considered 'reserves' or 'investments' by industry analysts, whenever more silver is available than the amount used by industry each year it is relegated to 'surplus'. And it is further assumed by analysts that when the silver price again rears its battered head toward double digit levels, that surplus will begin to come out of the woodwork, including the silver currently being carried around in India, even though there are government regulations about exporting this metal.

Demand

Unlike gold, which is primarily used to represent money, and whose main industrial use is in jewellery; silver is used for a myriad of industrial applications as well as fulfilling a time-tested role in the world as 'poor man's gold'. Because the largest industrial usage of silver involves photography, electronics, and many of the amenities of modern life in the free world, silver's demand may also be based on a demographic fundamental translated into annual consumption per capita in any specific area of the world. For example, during the 1970s, it became apparent to researchers that the western civilisation used far more silver to take pictures of friends, family and children than came forth from newly mined ore each year. This is but one example of photography demand. People living in the US, England and free Europe, let alone Japan, are increasingly attracted to other items that use silver such as TV colour sets, videocassette recorders, washing machines, computers. To these can be added other electric and electronic civilian and military gadgets and gimmicks that use silver, such as batteries containing silver oxide, which provide large bursts of dependable power for brief periods of time and are part of the Polaris missile propulsion system. Because of this the author has compiled a per capita annual silver demand parameter for the leading industrial nations in order to be able to translate into a reasonable yardstick this obvious demand factor for the amenities of American life so sought by residents of other nations – especially those in socialist countries. Table 7.1 reflects estimated current silver demand per person per year in major consuming countries.

Table 7.1 Estimated annual per capita silver demand

Country	1987 population	1987 silver use per person
US	238 million	0.6 oz. = 142 million oz.
USSR	350 million	0.5 oz. = 175 million oz.
China	1,200 million	0.05 oz. = 60 million oz.*

Source: The Metals Consultancy
Note: * = Metals Consultancy estimates include electronic and photographic materials containing silver purchased in Japan, US, etc.

The Metals Consultancy members are convinced that the amenities of American life, which gluttonously devour silver, will be increasingly demanded by the residents of socialist economies like the USSR and China. And it may be safe to assume that the bureaucrats in those countries will emphasise increased production of those items, such as washing machines, to prevent unrest amongst the peoples of their nations. For example, at the time of writing the number one priority of the People's Republic of China is to electrify the country. So that, if currently there are 15 million TV sets produced mainly by Chinese factories, there will soon be 100 million sets. In the United States, in 1986, there were 85 million TV sets. In China during 1987 several washing machine factories went into production with production targets set for hundreds of thousands of machines per year. And as a trade official proudly told the author some years ago, these efforts to produce TV sets, washing machines, cameras, film, etc. in China are basically to satisfy domestic demand, rather than to sell the merchandise in foreign markets. Assuming that annual silver demand in the United States will remain stagnant, or advance slightly toward the 0.75 silver ounce per person per year by the year 2000, and assuming that the silver demand in the USSR to the end of the current century also remains rather inflexible, the key rise in silver demand in the near future has to come out of China – even though silver chopsticks may by AD 2000 be considered capitalist luxury.

The Bureau of Mines in Washington closely monitors and publishes silver consumption in the United States. Table 7.2 is a table indicating

Table 7.2 US silver consumption by end use[1] (Thousands of troy ounces)

End use[2]	1986	1987	
		First quarter	Second quarter
Electroplated ware	3,724	757	757
Sterling ware	3,935	1,063	1,063
Jewellery	4,621	1,014	1,068
Photographic materials	55,449	(r)7,526	7,526
Dental and medical supplies	1,474	365	347
Mirrors	970	242	242
Brazing alloys and solders	6,432	(r)1,548	1,550
Electrical and electronic products:			
Batteries	3,722	1,510	1,510
Contacts and conductors	27,406	10,003	9,953
Bearings	375	120	94
Catalysts	2,313	959	972
Coins, medallions, and commemorative objects	3,957	675	627
Miscellaneous[3]	4,562	1,135	1,135
Total net industrial consumption[4]	118,940	(r)26,917	26,846
Coinage[5]	7,427	1,174	5,093
Total consumption[4]	126,367	(r)28,091	31,939

(r) Revised.
1. Data may include estimates.
2. End use as reported by converters of refined silver.
3. Includes silver-bearing copper, silver-bearing lead anodes, ceramic paints, etc.
4. Data may not add to totals shown because of independent rounding.
5. Includes silver used in minting the George Washington Commemorative Coin, the $1.00 Liberty Coin, and the American Eagle Bullion Coin.

American consumption of silver for the first two quarters of 1987 – and also the final figures for US silver use in 1986.

From the above table it becomes clear that the major sectors of silver use in the United States during 1986 were in order of importance: photography; electronics; coins; jewellery; and miscellaneous.

1 *Photography*: This sector includes colour, black and white, x-ray and industrial photography; graphic arts; and instant pictures such as those developed by Polaroid and Eastman Kodak. Historically, the photography sector dominates US silver usage, at times exceeding by far the newly mined silver from American mines each year. Annual demand for this fundamental in the US in excess of 60 million ounces might be considered bullish; annual US photography demand under 50 million ounces would be bearish.

2   *Electronics*: Since silver is one of the best conductors of both heat and
    electricity, and since the metal is malleable and ductile and lends
    itself to alloying with both base and precious metals, and since silver
    resists oxidation, it has been increasingly used in the electrical and
    electronics industries, in many differing applications from fuses,
    contacts, switching systems, in epoxy resins for circuit boards – even
    in powder form to mix with cement to carry current through
    sidewalks that can be electrically heated to melt snow. According to
    Shearson, the usage of silver for electronic purposes in Japan has
    been increasing, as well as it has been for other applications.
    Elsewhere silver is used in military electronics, space applications,
    medical and industrial systems. Of course, silver is used in
    videocassette recorders, computers, TVs, switches for washing
    machines and dishwashers, etc. But lumped all together, silver's
    demand factor for electrical and electronics applications normally
    lies in the area of total demand of 22 to 24 per cent.

3   *Coins*: At one time, the United States, Canada, Great Britain, and
    many other countries put silver in the money in circulation. Since
    the United States took the silver out of the money, most of the other
    nations followed suit. So that the coinage fundamental which was
    once the leading silver demand area dropped markedly in com-
    parison to silver's other commercial uses. But the success of selling
    proof silver coins for special occasions by government mints seems to
    have spurred a partial revival for silver coins in general. Moreover, in
    recent years, the issuance of legal-tender silver coins by nations such
    as the United States, Canada, Mexico, etc. obviously affects annual
    silver demand. Medallions issued by so-called 'private mints' in
    coin-like shapes also seem to be well received by small investors all
    over the globe. Details of the various legal tender silver coins minted
    by nations round the world may be found in the Silver Institute's
    annual publication *Modern Silver Coinage*. See Further reading,
    Appendix B.

4   *Jewellery*: Some of the most intricate and beautiful silver jewellery
    may be found in remote parts of China where women wear silver
    ornaments that clang as they dance to the music of a three-string
    Chinese guitar. In Central and South Amercia, silver in beads,
    necklaces, and ornaments reflect creativity and inventiveness.
        Since silver is much less expensive than gold, and since there is
    about nine times the amount of silver on earth than there is gold,
    and since for centuries silver in the form of coins has been available
    for fashioning decorative items, it is not at all surprising to find
    people almost everywhere wearing silver. The difference in modern
    countries between silver and gold jewellery is that the artist and

craftsman who designs jewellery has to be paid for labour. If a bracelet contains $100 worth of gold, when the cost of creation is added to the metal, percentagewise the final price is fairer to the buyer than if a bracelet containing $10 worth of silver were fashioned and the cost of design and manufacture were applied. One quick glance through any catalogue which sell jewellery mail-order clearly shows the dominance of gold jewellery over silver. Thus if there are ten pages of gold items, possibly a single page might be devoted to silver.

Sales of sterling place settings, and plated ware have declined for a variety of reasons, including the fact that items created from stainless steel do not have to be polished. Nor do steel pitchers turn dark brown or black from the formation of silver sulphide. Although there have been some serious attempts to produce tarnish-proof silver by dipping sterling in rhodium, the real success in that direction so far has been with sterling chains. Ironically, pure silver does not tarnish. But since the major portion of products sold as silver by jewellers is sterling, which is 92.5 per cent pure silver and 7.5 per cent copper, this alloy does tarnish when exposed to air containing sulphurous fumes. And to regain this lustre, the sterling must be polished properly, a rather demanding task in a servant-less civilisation.

Moreover, gold jewellery is heavily promoted, unlike silver, so its fascinating possibilities in decoration and jewellery have been virtually nil.

However, in 1987 the Silver Institute, whose members include silver mining interests in North America, Mexico and Peru, formed a Silver Producers Committee to probe the possibilities of promoting silver in its various forms. Initially, this group conducted a marketing study to determine where to place the emphasis of their promotion efforts on behalf of silver. If the group ever is adequately financed and promotes silver and its products in the proper direction, demand in this sector may rise from its current flat status to become a growth situation.

5   *Miscellaneous*: Lumped under the miscellaneous rubric are many significant uses of silver, in batteries – with military uses and implications. In hearing aids, cameras, calculators, watches and clocks. Silver is used in both pacemakers for heart problems and fuel cells used in space. As a key component in brazing and soldering alloys, silver is required when copper tubing is to be joined together. Silver is also used as a catalyst in certain organic chemical applications. Medically it has become famous for its bactericidal attributes, being used in diverse items from burn cream to middle ear

and penis implantations to water purification. Silver's use in optical fibres has opened up a whole new field for the metal, as has its application in solar cells. Indeed, readers who may be interested in following new developments in silver's experimental future might like to subscribe to *New Silver Technology*, prepared and published by the Silver Institute. Although there are many current uses of silver that have not been mentioned, such as in mirrors and plating, glass and ceramics, the important thing to remember is that experimentation has a long road to run before commercial application. So in the meantime, the silver price will continue to be affected by the demand fundamentals mentioned.

IMPACT OF FUNDAMENTALS ON THE SILVER PRICE

By way of background, since the end of World War II, the United States, a leading silver producing country, has never produced more than about a third of its silver demand. The silver that has made up the deficit between what the United States produces each year and what its industrialised economy requires, has been made up of recycled items such as coin melt, and silver bars and concentrates imported from other countries. In the meantime, since the end of the war industrial growth has been encountered in Germany and Japan, among the free market countries; the USSR and China, among the managed market nations. When attempting to assess the fundamentals detailed above and their impact on the going price, the silver price herein will be US dollars. Table 7.3 is intended to reflect action and reaction of the silver price to the changing fundamentals, dollarwise.

Although changes in the fundamentals mentioned above could cause price action and reaction, changes in technical assessment by traders and speculators along with changing in hedging needs may alter the price situation somewhat.

FINDING SILVER FUNDAMENTALS

The first fundamental needed is the silver price. During trading hours, unless one is actually in the silver pits or hooked up to a bullion source, this is generally supplied through the video screens of information services, such as Reuters, Quotron, etc. Services such as Comtrend supply not only videos but also printouts so that a trader can track prices during futures trading sessions. Of course, the silver price in physical markets also appears on the electronic screens of various bullion sources and brokers. And if the trader or speculator does not have a computer nor leases information services of a video nature, the prices in the

Table 7.3 Impact of changing fundamentals on silver price

Bullish impact:
1. increased industrial consumption
2. increased investment demand
3. decreased new mine production
4. decreased refined silver stocks
5. decreased exchange silver stocks
6. increased population
7. increased silver jewellery purchases
8. increased inflation
9. increase in the gold price
10. depreciation of the dollar *vs* strong currencies
11. publication of new silver technology in industry
12. publication of new silver technology in health
13. central bank purchases for coinage and medals

Bearish impact:
1. decreased industrial consumption
2. decreased investor activity
3. increased new mine production
4. increased recycled silver
5. increased refined silver stocks
6. increased exchange silver stocks
7. decreased jewellery manufacture and purchase
8. decreased inflation
9. decrease in the gold price
10. appreciation of the dollar *vs* strong currencies
11. decreased central bank purchases for mintings

various markets can be seen in newspapers with financial sections, such as the *Financial Times, Wall Street Journal, New York Times,* etc.

Exchange stocks and their levels may be monitored daily via sheets sent by the exchange to members who service the public as well as those who trade for themselves and for other members. In the absence of being able to obtain the daily sheets, weekly reportage of these stocks appears in the financial press, especially in the *American Metal Market.* American silver production and consumption, imports and exports are monitored by the Bureau of Mines, Washington DC, an agency that produces annual mineral summaries, which include silver among other metals. The Bureau publishes a monthly bulletin entitled *Gold and Silver Monthly,* which contains important fundamental information about both silver and gold.

Research companies such as CRU (Consolidated Research Unit) in London and Rosskill in Ireland publish studies of a fundamental nature about metals, including silver. McGraw-Hill publishes *Metals Week* providing concise coverage of base and precious metals numbers and events; and the same publisher issues *Engineering & Mining* monthly, which covers all metals and provides an annual assessment of silver fundamentals and their changes. Bullion firms, such as Sharps-Pixley, publish an annual silver review, as does Shearson in London. Brokerage firms that have precious metals departments issue from time to time reviews of gold and silver. And the author has contributed a monthly column entitled 'NY Hotline' to the *Nikkei Letter*, the precious metals letter of the *Nihon Keizai Shimbun* (Japan Economic Journal). The most widely read and respected annual silver publication is the *Handy & Harman Silver Review*, which is free to interested participants in the silver milieu. The 1987 review revealed silver purchases by China and the USSR, and silver exports from India, as well as the most comprehensive assessment of silver supply/demand from non-Communist countries.

The exchanges that trade silver futures and options on silver futures will gladly send free literature to interested readers. COMEX is located at 4 World Trade Center, New York, NY 10048. CBOT is at 141 W. Jackson Boulevard, Chicago, Illinois 60604. The Tokyo Commodity Exchange For Industry, which trades in 10-kilo silver futures (320 oz) – with a minimum of 30 kilos for delivery – is located at Tosen Building, 10−8 Horidome 1-chome, Nihonbashi, Chuo-ku, Tokyo, Japan. And the Sydney (Australia) Futures Exchange Ltd is located on the 7th floor, Australia Square Tower, Sydney 2000.

Armed with the above information, traders and speculators who desire to do their own fundamental research can assemble some meaningful facts for possible market action. Incidentally, the annual reports of publicly traded firms, such as Coeur d'Alene Mines, Callahan, Hecla, Asarco, etc. usually contain a silver review along with some sort of expectations of silver's fortunes for the year ahead. Of course, financial magazines all over the world, from *Forbes* to *Business Week* to *Fortune* and the *Economist* feature from time to time cogent articles on silver, as does the *Financial World*, in New York. But alas the price of silver does not only depend on promising or depressing fundamentals. That price depends on the actions of diverse groups in the various silver markets, physical and paper.

In this regard a technical assessment of the silver price must also be arrived at in order to conceive both the long-term and short-term postures of the market.

TECHNO-FUNDAMENTALS

By now it should be readily inferred that to make an intelligent trading decision in the silver market it is necessary to know the fundamental situation in the metal. If the fundamentals are going to improve appreciably in the foreseeable future, the fundamental picture is basically bullish. If the fundamentals are going to further pressure the price, profits may be made via short sales or put purchases.

But there are multitudes of speculators and traders who are firmly convinced that the fundamentals are already in the going market price of the metal. Advances in price, therefore, will indicate increasingly favourable supply/demand silver fundamentals; whilst silver price collapses occur because the fundamantals are dramatically gloomy. So, whereas from one viewpoint silver is seen as fundamentally under-valued to gold, technically oriented traders have no such concepts. Instead they are interested in assessing whether silver will rise or fall in price in the future based upon assessment derived from a technical charting system or other strategies which analyse the past price movement and whatever other ingredients, such as volume, open-interest, option action, even action of soyabeans. The next chapter is aimed at helping those technically oriented traders to familiarise themselves with a charting or other technical system (or a computer program or model, if need be) to confirm their feelings about the silver markets and to aid decisions to trade the metal from the long or the short side.

8

SILVER TECHNICAL RESEARCH

While silver fundamentals gravitate around changes in supply and demand for the metal, technical assessment involves those factors that influence the market price, mainly in the short term. Of course, there are long-term price forecasting theories such as the Elliot wave theory and these will be expanded upon in the next chapter on silver trading systems (see page 102). But right here it is necessary to reflect on short-term movements in silver.

SILVER SHORT-TERM PRICE MOVEMENTS

In order for the owner of a long or short position in a gold future on COMEX to gross $500 on that position, the gold futures price would have to move up or down $5 ($5 x 100 oz). In order for a silver futures long or short trader to gross $500 on the position, the silver futures price would have to only advance or decline by 10 cents ($0.10 x 5,000 oz). A one cent move in a silver future on COMEX is equivalent to a gross move up or down of $50; and a 20-cent move = a gross of $1,000.

The technically oriented silver trader monitors price movements of the volatile markets in silver by referring to some sort of chart. Fig. 8.1 represents bar chart price movement in silver based on a 10-cent variation; and Fig. 8.2 represents a bar chart of silver with 20-cent intervals.

These charts are constructed with bars indicating the high, low and closing silver price being charted. Chart watchers using such records of past price movements connect tops, bottoms and sometimes middles of their bars to establish trend lines. They then usually extend those lines to depict a specific price target. Fig. 8.3 illustrates this aspect of past price examination coupled with future price expectation.

In addition to bar charts, which may also include such factors as volume and open interest, there are point-and-figure charts, which do not consider the time factor at all, nor any other factor except price patterns and their reversals. Some wags call this financial tic-tac-toe

SILVER DEC 1987 COMEX
EACH HORIZONTAL LINE = 10.00 CENTS
TRADING HOURS: 8:25-2:25 EST
HIGH: 1014.80 ON 04/27/87
LOW: 543.50 ON 05/20/86

Source: Commodity Research Bureau

Fig. 8.1 Silver price in 10-cent intervals

('noughts and crosses') because the crosses signify rising prices and the noughts signify declining ones – with changes from x's to o's and vice versa only when the selected price differential interval has been reached or breached. Fig. 8.4 is illustrative of a point figure chart.

Another matter of depicting silver's price past in order to foresee its future on a technical basis, involves innovation deriving from the Japanese pole system of charting. This system depicts daily action by indicating to the viewer the opening and closing prices – and also the high and low range for the day. Up-days are coloured red and down-days black, so the observer can readily depict the past. Moreover, this

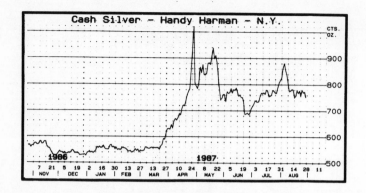

Source: Commodity Research Bureau

Fig. 8.2 Silver price in 20-cent intervals

type of chart has hairlines which help the viewer form an opinion of
what should happen during the next trading day. Figure 8.5 reflects a
silver pole chart.

Appendix A at the back of this book lists representative firms that
supply charting services and other technical price depicting services.
Constructing charts is for many people merely an entertaining exercise
but the chances are that serious traders will eventually hit on a system of
charting suitable to their own needs and market decisions.

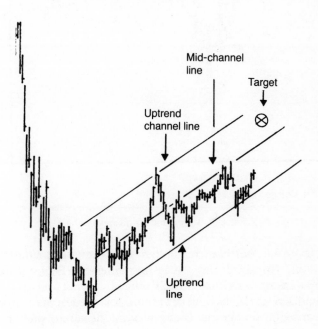

Source: Thomson McKinnon

Fig. 8.3 Illustration of trend lines on a bar chart

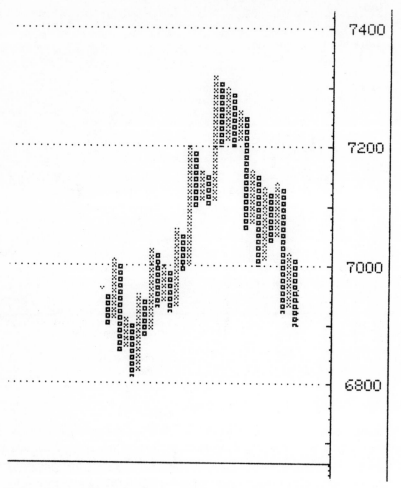

Source: Chicago Board of Trade

Fig. 8.4 Silver point and figure chart

In this regard, constructing the chart is an exercise in 20/20 hindsight. Interpreting the chart and forecasting where the silver price will go tomorrow or next week are entirely other arts, if not precisely 'sciences'.

Quite often technical traders become absorbed in areas that are not too meaningful on the price one way or the other, such as tracking volume, which is a measure of liquidity rather than price direction. But tracking open interest, the statistic that represents buys and sells together of silver futures, is something else.

DOJI line after a long red line
an indicator that we are at, or
near, a ceiling

Three consecutive black
lines forecast lower prices

A DOJI line – turning period in the
market—followed by consecutive reds,
forecast higher prices

JUNE 1

JULY 6

Source: Steven Sarnoff

Fig. 8.5 Silver pole chart

The interpretation of changes in open interest (the number of combined buy/sell positions in silver not liquidated during an exchange trading session but remaining open in position) involves four different market situations.

1 *Open interest rises and silver price rises*: In this event, it is believed that the market contains momentum for a further rise in the silver price.
2 *Open interest falls and silver price rises*: Here the silver price may be facing an imminent reversal in direction.
3 *Open interest rises and silver price falls*: Technicians believe in this situation that there is momentum for a further decline in the silver price.
4 *Open interest declines and silver price falls*: In this case it is broadly believed that the downward pattern will encounter a reversal and turn upward.

In addition to simple technical approaches to silver price forecasting such as chart construction and interpretation, econometric approaches utilising computer models are growing popular. Since most of these trading models rely upon examination of regressions, multiple regressions, and other statistical esoterica, the reader who is mathematically oriented in both statistics and calculus would do well to purchase a copy of Jack Schwager's book, *A Complete Guide to the Futures Markets* (see Further reading, Appendix B). In this comprehensive work the author, research director of futures for Prudential Bache, not only explains and develops technical systems and trading models, but also provides an eclectic – and understandable – review of econometrics. But in the primer for the silver trader being presented here we are trying to cover a complicated subject with the minimum of complexities. So having presented open interest in just such a fashion, along with several popular types of charts it is time to move on to other technical factors that affect price movements in silver in the paper and the physical markets.

A look at the past action on any kind of a silver chart indicates intervals where the price fluctuates back and forth over a period of time between a ceiling that it fails to penetrate called 'resistance' and a floor it fails to fall through labelled 'support'. This is the trading range. If the price suddenly rises above the resistance level, this eruption is called a 'breakout'. Continuation of the rising price thereafter may result in a sharp drop forming a 'spike'. For example, on Friday 24 April 1987, COMEX nearby silver closed at $9.04. On Monday, 27 April the contract rose up to $11.25, dropped as low as $7.50 and closed with the May delivery at $8.29. Some chartists on that Monday concluded on a technical basis that if silver broke out over $12 it could rise quickly to $20. Later that day they also concluded if it dropped below $7 it could drop to $4.

In addition to watching price patterns on charts for areas violating support and resistance, technicians interpret various patterns as meaningful indicators of trends. Included in these patterns are such formations as tops and bottoms, double tops and bottoms, triple tops and bottoms, heads and shoulders, flags and pennants, triangles, rising and falling wedges, etc. Price formations are, of course, thereafter interpreted as bullish or bearish according ot the pattern produced. In addition to simply charting the price, many technicians also chart moving averages of the silver price, using various time periods, 10-day, 20-day, 30-day averages, etc. Some technicians plot the moving average of their choice on the same chart as their price depiction, generally using a differently coloured ink for the moving average and black for the price reflections. And since the moving average rises toward or falls away from the current silver price, when the paths meet, or cross or diverge, signals are sent to the technician to take specific market action.

In recent years cyclical movements in commodities have caused creation of charts that depict buy/sell signals from anticipated changes in the price cycle. Briefly, the cyclical representations are *rounded* representations of variations of bar charts. According to those who use cyclical charts in connection with silver trading, these are so-called 'timing tools'.

TECHNICAL TIMING IN SILVER TRADING

On any business day, the silver price in the paper world may fluctuate enough during the trading session in the futures pits to rack up profits and losses for short-term speculators and trading professionals. Success in short-term trading, therefore, depends upon a number of factors, including: (a) speed of entering and exiting the market; (b) ability to foresee the price direction within profitable limits, if day trading; (c) limiting greed to specified areas, such as number of silver contracts to risk; and (d) cutting losses quickly, if wrong.

Given the above conditions – and adding very low transaction costs – silver traders on the scene of the action have a decided edge over those in office. One of the big pluses for those near the pits involves watching who is buying and selling – and which way the action will dominate: i.e. sellers over buyers or vice versa.

Since October 1984, COMEX has also had active trading in options on its silver futures. Since the risk-takers who hit the bids for these puts and calls on silver futures often resort to buying or selling silver futures for coverage of their options risks, action in the options ring can signal feverish action in the futures pit, etc.

Assume that a trader is satisfied with a 5-cent move in the silver price as a day-trade target, which means the long or the short position will be closed out before the trading session ends. Further assume that because of signals sent to him from the charts he uses to confirm market decisions, the trader would rather be long than short as his market entry. When should he go long? On weakness to later liquidate on market strength? The chances are that such a tactic for a day trade would result in losses rather than profits. The time to go long would be when a move has already started in the pits causing the price to begin to rise – and then liquidate the position before the clamour for more long contracts reaching the pits ends. Of course, the trader might have missed the cream of a 20- or 30-cent intra-day upward move. But his original target was 5 cents, and once that target was reached why try a further spin of the wheel of fortune?

Contrarians, of course, would go long on weakness and sell on strength, meaning precisely the opposite action from small public speculators. But here again the need for proper timing in placing buy and sell orders separates the experienced from the novice. Actually it doesn't matter to a trader seeking small or moderate profits which direction the long-term trend of the silver price is travelling as long as it fluctuates up and down enough for the traders to attain realistic, if modest, gain over and above their transaction costs.

In addition to using charts as props for trading decisions, trading models that rely on a statistical equation programmed into a computer may be called into play. Computerised programs are increasingly being used to trade in silver options. The software used to evaluate silver options on futures, for example, not only provide fair value, over-value and undervalue of option premiums being traded; but also may provide the Greek that is prevalent in option trading such as the delta, the beta, the gamma, etc. Usage of properly constructed computer software is often essential in deciding which silver options to sell naked, covered, or half-covered. And, of course, a computer model on the silver price that works fairly well could be of enormous assistance to silver speculators and hedgers. In the next chapter the major elements of a silver trading model will be touched upon and explained. Right now a brief mention of gaps and shocks.

When the silver market surges up or down on the opening far above or below the closing price of the previous session, a gap is created on bar charts. If the gap is an upside breakaway one that is not filled by a receding price in the next few trading sessions, it is considered a rather strong buy signal. Conversely if there is a downside gap in the silver price chart formation, and that is not filled by an upward reaction within a few trading sessions following the downside breakthrough of the support level, then that gap is a strong signal for shorting the futures. There are, of course, other interpretations of gaps; and these can be found in specialised technical literature.

9

SILVER SYSTEMS AND PLANNING

The fire engine-red BMW flashing down the highway toward the World Trade Center in New York each trading day bears the licence plates 'SILVER 2'. This doesn't mean that the trader driving the new car bought silver at $2 and used profits to pay for the vehicle. It means that $2 is the price where he will change his system of trading. Until silver drops to that level the trader will go short on strength and cover on weakness. This kind of intuitive trading system may be jeered at or derided by those versed in computer lore, in statistics and mathematics. But there are records of intuitive trading systems that have worked quite well. There even once was a system that dictated that the price of silver followed soya beans, or vice versa, perhaps, because at one time Hunt Bros. were trading in soya beans as well as silver.

The tendency on the part of brokerage and bullion firms to resort to price projection based upon fundamental and technical analysis; and for traders to act long or short because of signals generated by various kinds of systems is quite understandable. If money is made that way, it is done with knowledge; and if money is lost at least there had to be a logical reason; the variables weren't correct; the statistics were wrongly interpreted, etc.

In this regard, techicians seem to have fixed upon the following four major categories of trading systems; trend-following; price change rate; contrarian and pattern action.

TREND-FOLLOWING SYSTEMS

As the silver price travels from 31 December each year to the first trading day in January of the coming year and the 31 December of that year price trends are established. Silver traders seem to be more interested in the short-term trend than the long-term. But to follow the trends the astute silver trader never tries to catch the top or the bottom of a move. Instead, when a price move begins in the pits reflecting a rise and the user of this method decides to go long (buy) for an intra-day turn, he will normally wait a while until he sees the move really started and then jump in. As the price rises (if it is a one-day trade) the trader will either place a trailing stop order to sell, or simply exit the market at a profit.

If the trend-following silver trader sees a downward movement developing he waits until it is confirmed, according to his predetermined sell-points and then goes short. Should the price continue to decline he then – if it is a day-trade – may insert a trailing buy stop order, or simply buy to cover and establish the profit.

For traders who are not interested in short-term up and down moves, but hungry to retrieve substantial profits, a 'position' is accumulated, which may or may not be protected with either stop orders or protective options. In any event if the position (more than one silver long or short) proves profitable according to the trend-following methods used, the position can either be enlarged or reduced, according to the risks the trader is willing to assume.

Users of trend-following systems usually resort to trading either with checks upon moving averages, or in the wake of breakouts.

A moving average may be ten days, twenty days, or as long as the trader desires. To calculate the moving average, assume it's a twenty-day one, the closing price for each of the twenty days is averaged and divided by twenty to attain an average price for that time period. On the next trading session close, the constructor of the moving average deletes the first date's price and adds the close of the current session and averages the resulting twenty days, etc. In this manner, the twenty-day moving average when placed on a chart displaying daily price action in silver will lag – and be below the current price path – if silver is rising; and, of course, if the current price is declining, the moving average plotted on the same chart will appear above the current price path, etc. It's when the moving average and the price cross each other that trading signals appear.

In theory, a buy signal in silver is assumed to be generated when the current price path crosses the moving average from below; and a sell signal is assumed to be generated when the price path of the current silver market crosses the moving average from above.

Another variation of the trend-following cognoscenti involves action on breakouts. As previously explained, a breakout occurs when the price path of silver erupts beyond the trendlines signifying resistance and support. In such cases, usually the breakout provides momentum for further appreciation of the price or further decline, as the case may be.

But as in so many other systematic approaches to silver trading, there are often problems such as (a) the interval for the moving average is either too short or too long; (b) too many traders may be using the same guidelines to act in the market; (c) major price moves may be missed in the main; (d) there may be excessive monetary losses via being whipsawed or stopped out frequently; and (e) volatility may wipe out profits.

PRICE RATE CHANGE SYSTEM

In its simplest concept, price rate change involves examination of rising and falling markets to determine when the rate of price change is declining. For example, before a rising price can reverse and turn downward its rate of change upwards has to decline; and the converse is true in the case of a falling market that will turn around, but before it does its rate of decline will be reduced. When plotted properly the curve crossings should indicate bottoms or tops in relation to price direction.

CONTRARIAN SYSTEMS

While technicians rely on such esoteric items as oscillators (measures of momentum) to set up confirmation for employment of the contrarian approach to profits in silver, the basic tenets of this approach involve the concept that whenever speculators are basically bullish and the price has soared, it will be difficult to attract new speculators to keep the price high if these older bullish speculators want to unload. The famous maxim 'They can't all get out by the same door' seems to work whenever the silver price has an unusual rise. Thus in effect contrarians are traders who practise the belief that the public is always wrong. For mathematicians or statisticians interested in exploring the avenues of coming up with a contrary opinion re any commodity price, there is a storehouse of professional literature available, some of which is mentioned in Appendix A.

PATTERN ACTION

Evidently it is necessary for users of trend-following systems to seek confirmation via patterns formed by (a) the current silver price path; (b) the silver price path and the moving averages or other paths traced on the same chart; and/or (c) the time required for the signal set up by the pattern to be confirmed.

Thus if the silver price made a pennant signifying a possible direction in the future price of the metal, one of the rules the systems user might make is that the signal has to last for at least three days before it is 'confirmed'.

The creation of a statistical model that involves a regression equation may be a bit difficult when it comes to creating a model to predict prices of silver futures or options on silver futures, since the average silver future runs about 18 months – with only about six months or less of that period being actively traded. Instead, it might make sense to create a silver pricing model on physical silver, which could by modification of the price prediction represented by the dependent variable provide a ball-park number for any particular silver future being traded.

Many years ago Intergold commissioned Eugene Sherman, an economist, to create a gold pricing model. And it is recommended that anyone who desires to attempt a silver pricing model obtain a copy of Sherman's book, *Gold Investment Theory and Application*, (see Further reading, Appendix B). Basically gold is affected in its going price by at least twenty eight different pressures, fundamental and political, as well as investment and speculative action. But if the silver price is the dependent variable in a regression model then the independent variables are not nearly as many as in gold. In a 1975 analysis entitled *A Methodology for Price Forecasting*, Walter Myers, former Research Director at ContiCommodity Services proposed the following basics on which any commodity price model is to be constructed:

1 Define a specific real world problem of importance before undertaking the analysis.
2 Gain an understanding of the economic mechanism which generated the problem and influences its solution.
3 Acquire a knowledge of the underlying time varying properties of the series itself.
4 Select the minimum number of parameters and data transformations necessary for describing the situation before estimating the coefficients.

Myers concluded: 'Not only do users not understand complicated econometric models, but complicated models generally break down over time. In fact there's much to be gained from a thorough understanding of the pricing mechanism and correctly identifying the two or three major factors influencing the market than there is in building elaborate estimating techniques'. He further suggested: 'Market decisions are made for a specific market price in a particular time period. Having constructed the linear equation which constitutes the pricing model, it is necessary to test statistically and empirically evaluate the estimating performance of the model'.

A linear silver pricing model would appear as an equation:

$$Y = a + \beta_1 X_1 + \beta_2 X_2 + \beta_3 X_3 \ldots .$$

Since the silver physical prices, such as the daily London fixing, go back for many years, it is suggested that researchers who wish to construct a pricing model only go back to the end of 1974, when both gold and silver were in a free market in the US and gold and silver had some sort of correlation as to price direction. For readers without a broad statistical or mathematical background it is suggested that they refer to Jack Schwager's *A Complete Guide to the Commodity Markets* which has chapters on most of the major aspects of constructing a pricing model using regressional analysis and statistical theory. The three most important variables when it comes to the silver price are annual silver supply; annual silver demand; and annual perceptions of investors and speculators. And naturally there are other figures that could be used in a silver pricing formula as parameters for the independent variables. But whatever numbers are used in constructing the silver price model, one way of checking the efficacy of the model is to see if the model can come up with the silver price for back years if the variables for those years are inserted into the formula. If they cannot approach a fair amount of accuracy something is either missing or has been logged in incorrectly. But if the model comes up with fairly close prices for each past period, the theory is that it should be able to project future silver prices according to changes foreseen in the independent variables, etc.

TRADING THE GOLD/SILVER RATIO

Although much ado has been made about trading methods and systems that rely on charts, computers, formulae, etc. there is still an awful lot to be said in favour of trading the gold/silver ratio.

Basically, when the cost of buying one ounce of gold in terms of selling silver ounces exceeds a certain area, then silver is undervalued to gold. So that the trader, not knowing or caring if precious metals prices will rise or fall in the future is merely interested in profiting on either the widening or the narrowing of the premium in terms of silver ounces over that metal by the price of gold.

For example, for four hundred years from 1500 to 1900 it took only an average of about 15 ounces of silver sold in the market to buy one ounce of gold. And for the past century, it has taken an average of 33 silver ounces to buy one gold ounce. But as this book is being completed it takes 70 ounces of silver to buy one ounce of gold. That is why – at least in the author's opinion – silver is greatly undervalued to gold. Now the widest premium the author has ever heard of when it comes to this gold/silver ratio is about 90 to 1 of silver to gold. And the lowest premium in modern times existed in January, 1980 when the ratio had narrowed down to about 17 silver to gold.

At the time of writing there is a growing group of market analysts who claim silver and gold have gone their separate ways and have no relationship to each other any more. Another set of analysts claim the only game in town is gold, which will go to unimaginably high dollar prices because of future inflation, etc. Yet, the gold/silver ratio has been a part of history for centuries. And one of the fascinating aspects of history is that is periodically repeats itself. The ratio can be played in the physical market by holders of gold selling the metal and putting the proceeds into silver when the ratio is wide, as at the time of writing. Then when the ratio narrows, the silver can be sold and the proceeds reinvested into gold.

In the silver and gold paper markets, the ratio can be played with options and with futures or combined. For example, an investor can go long a silver future for say twelve months hence and simultaneously go short a gold future on a basis of one 5,000-ounce contract of silver long for every 100-ounce gold contract short. Or the risk-taker can go long a silver call and simultaneously go long a gold put for the same expiration dates. Or the trader can go long a silver future and long a gold put; or short a gold future and long a silver call. Depending, of course, on where the premiums for the options are at time of trades.

OTHER SILVER TRADING STRATEGIES

In the above example of assuming silver is undervalued to gold, so that silver is bought and gold is sold, similar thinking may be applied to other metals, which may be over-valued to the going silver price. For example, when copper prices are high, a trader might try going long silver futures and shorting copper futures. Or he might go long silver futures or bullion and buy puts on copper. Or calls on silver could be bought and puts on copper could be bought, etc.

Since silver in physical form is bulky, expensive to store and insure, costly to transfer and ship, and ties up capital when held for long periods of time in portfolio, the owners of such silver might want to avail themselves of a regular cash flow by continually selling (writing) covered silver calls on COMEX or the CBOT. Actually there are many option strategies available to silver traders who desire to seek profits with protection. For example, a bullish silver speculator likes May 1988 silver, goes long the future and sells a covered call. If the silver price rises, the seller has profited by the premium (less transaction charges); and if silver declines, the seller may be able to buy his open short call back for a pittance and wait for a rise to sell another covered call, etc. If the price of silver drops instead of rises, the holder of the long future has downside protection only to the amount of the premium, but he's still positioned his silver cheaper than anyone else on the day of market entry who did not sell a covered call.

The arcane art of option selling on silver and on gold futures has developed into a blossoming area – with software to help the interested speculator and trader make market decisions. These computer aids present fair value of any silver option, the delta of the option (its hedge ratio), and other guides. Software Options, pioneers in that area, have developed through their COTS division sophisticated measures such as the gamma. Fig. 9.1 illustrates an explanation of the gamma.

Recently Software Options (address at rear of book in Appendix A) has developed for IBM computers a floppy disk called *FX Options Tutor* which comes with an instruction book. The package includes strategies that illustrate how silver options, futures or forward trades, and combinations of those trades can be used to capitalise on any market situation or risk-taker point-of-view to earn income, minimise risk or hedge an open position. Table 9.1 illustrates these possibilities.

THE ELLIOT WAVE THEORY

Believing that prices, like waves washing on to an ocean beach, rise and recede, followers of the Elliot Wave Theory applied to trading in silver are sincerely convinced that the price moves in three major movements upwards (interrupted by two minor down-moves) and then encounters a downward reversal of three major waves (interrupted by two minor up-moves). In other words, each section of a typical Elliot wave pattern is composed of five movements. Theorists who follow this system of price patterns separate the price rise as one cycle and the subsequent price fall as another cycle. The current grand panjandrum of this cult is Robert Prechter, publisher of the *Elliot Wave Theorist*, who has been predicting that gold is in its declining phase and is heading for $150 an ounce.

Without detracting from the accuracy or usefulness of this theory or of any of its offshoots that are found in the multitude of market letters huckstered to the information-hungry speculating public, in the final analysis, it's people who make prices, not computers, or systems or wave theories. There have arisen in recent years a multitude of technical indicators that measure 'sentiment', suggesting that silver may be over-bought or oversold; there are momentum indicators used by theorists who claim that if silver gets to $8 it will leap to $10, etc; just as there are chartists who volunteer that if silver breaks $6 it will drop to $4, etc.

But we would be remiss if in the midst of technical analysis the genuine secret to riches with silver is not revealed. And that secret is simply to *accumulate*, rather than speculate.

Gamma

Gamma is a statistic that measures the instantaneous rate of change of an option's delta with respect to underlying price. Gamma is the second derivative of the option theoretical value with respect to underlying price; it is the first derivative of the delta.

Gamma is used to provide an indication of how sensitive an option's delta is to underlying price changes. The higher the value of gamma, the more rapid the change in delta. Consequently, more attention must be given to rehedging a *high gamma* position than a *low gamma* position.

The following are characteristics of gamma:

1. Gamma increases as time to expiration decreases.

2. For a given maturity, at-market options have higher gammas than out-of-the-money options.

3. Gammas for call and put options having the same maturity and strike price are approximately the same.

4. Gamma decreases as volatility increases (for medium to long-term options only; that is, where time decay doesn't overwhelm other factors).

5. Gamma is of concern mainly for short options; that is, options sold or written.

To avoid confusion concerning the currency pricing unit of an option, gamma should be calculated based on a percentage move of the underlying price rather than an absolute move.

Just as a delta equivalent position is determined by multiplying the face amount of an option by its delta, a gamma position is calculated by multiplying the face amount of an option by its gamma. It

is then possible to sum the individual gamma positions and determine an overall gamma position for a portfolio. Note that gamma for a future or forward position is zero.

A risk inherent in writing options on relatively low volatility instruments, such as currencies, is that the change of the delta can be very rapid once an option is in the money. This can be illustrated graphically: the following diagram shows the curve of put option fair value vs underlying instrument price in three cases: a zero-volatility instrument, a low-volatility instrument and a high volatility instrument.

In the case of a zero-volatility instrument, the option has no time value; its fair value is either 0 or intrinsic value. And there is no transition in the delta; it is either 0 or 1. The option curve is not a curve at all, but two straight lines that intersect at the strike price.

With a low volatility instrument, the out-of-the-money portion of the curve is quite flat. Although there is a transition from the curve to the diagonal intrinsic value line, it occurs over a very small range of underlying price movement. Thus the gamma is high and the delta rises rapidly from, say, 0.6 to 1.0.

In the case of a high-volatility instrument, the gamma is relatively low. The delta moves smoothly and gradually from zero to 1.0.

The higher the volatility, the lower the gamma as the option moves from being out of the money to in the money, and the easier it is to adjust one's position to be fully hedged. Conversely, the lower the volatility, the higher the gamma as the option moves from being out of the money to in the money, and the more difficult it is for the trader to maintain a balanced position.

Courtesy: Software Options Corp.

Fig. 9.1 Explanation of the gamma of an option

Table 9.1 Silver option strategies

Point of view	Strategy	Risk	Profit potential
Strongly bullish	Buy call	Limited to premium paid	Unlimited
	Buy future/fwd, buy put (buy covered put)	Limited to option time value plus out of the money amount	Unlimited
	Buy future/fwd	Unlimited	Unlimited
Mildly bullish	Sell put	Unlimited	Limited to premium recd
	Buy future/fwd, sell call (covered call write)	Unlimited	Limited to option time value plus out of the money amount
	Buy call vertical spread	Limited to net premium paid	Limited to difference between strikes less premium paid
	Sell put vertical spread	Limited to difference between strikes less net premium recd	Limited to net premium recd
Stable	Put ration spread	Limited to net premium paid if market rises; unlimited if market falls	Limited to difference between strikes less net premium paid
	Sell straddle	Unlimited	Limited to premium recd
	Call ratio write	Unlimited	Limited to premium recd
	Put ratio write	Unlimited	Limited to premium recd
	Call calendar spread	Limited to net premium paid	Limited
	Put calendar spread	Limited to net premium paid	Limited
	Call ratio spread	Limited to net premium paid if market falls; unlimited if market rises	Limited to difference between strikes less net premium paid
Volatile	Buy straddle	Limited to premium paid	Unlimited
Mildly bearish	Sell call	Unlimited	Limited to premium recd
	Sell future/fwd, sell put (covered put write)	Unlimited	Limited to option time value plus out of the money amount
	Buy put vertical spread	Limited to net premium paid	Limited to difference between strikes less net premium paid

Table 9.1 Silver option strategies *continued*

Point of view	Strategy	Risk	Profit potential
	Sell call vertical spread	Limited to difference between strikes less net premium recd	Limited to premium recd
Strongly bearish	Buy put	Limited to premium paid	Unlimited
	Sell future/fwd, buy call (buy covered call)	Limited to option time value plus out of the money amount	Unlimited
	Sell future/fwd	Unlimited	Unlimited

SILVER ACCUMULATION

When the investor considers that the price is right, for example, below the cost of production in the United States, silver can be purchased in convenient coin or wafer forms from a variety of sources, including the US Mint and agents of the Royal Mint of Canada. It can be accumulated via regular purchases at banks and stock brokers offering such services. And the benefits of dollar averaging (buying an equal dollar amount during times when the price is rising and falling) which will eventually provide more silver for the personal stockpile than an equal amount of money invested in mathematically equal ounces. Table 9.2 illustrates this aspect of dollar-averaging with silver:

Table 9.2 Dollar averaging with silver

Silver price	# Fixed ounce	# Fixed $	# ounce
$5	100	$700	140
$6	100	$700	113
$7	100	$700	100
$8	100	$700	87
$9	100	$700	77
—	—	—	—
	500	$3,500	517

Inspection of the above table indicates that the mathematical averager who bought 100 ounces of silver at prices rising from $5 to $9 received for a $3,500 risk 500 silver ounces. The dollar-averager, using the same $3,500, but split into $700 intervals for each purchase price came out with 517 ounces. Dollar averaging works whether the price goes up or down. Assuming that both accumulators ended their market investments when silver was $9 an ounce, the gross investment of $3,500 would have been worth $4,500 for the averager, but for the dollar-averager it would have been a gross liquidating value of $4,653. Taking the worst possible scenario, that at the end of the five investment periods silver suddenly plunged back to $5 an ounce and both investors liquidated, the mathematical averager would have recouped $2,500 gross, whilst the dollar averager would have recouped a gross of $2,585. And if the silver price were $7 at time of liquidation, the mathematical averager would have broken even before charges, whilst the dollar averager would have recovered a gross of $3,619.

10

THE FUTURE FOR SILVER –
A PERSONAL VIEW

Investors traditionally have emulated the original Baron Rothschild who traded in animals 'buying sheep and selling deer'. But with the advent of the electronic age of instant communication and price discovery, many traders have made fortunes in silver when markets dropped as well as soared. The key question everyone seems anxious to have answered really is split into two parts: what will silver do in the short term; and what will the price be in the long term?

In the short term the silver price will fluctuate. But in the long term the author is perhaps stubbornly convinced that silver will not only again soar in value, but may even exceed the $50 an ounce all–time high for the metal achieved in January 1980.

Now before calling for the men in the white coats to take the author away to a padded cell kindly spend a few minutes to peruse the following. The basic thrust behind my unwavering belief that silver, like Phoenix from the ashes, will again rise significantly, does not involve visions of hyperinflation, disappearance of paper currency, or any of the other economic reasons for this precious metal to go back into being money. My reasoning involves centrally an anticipated explosive demand that is going to come from Communist, Socialist and third world countries, whose population want the amenities of life familiar to residents of the western world, who take TVs, VCRs, computers, washing machines, dryers, etc. for granted.

And as mentioned in Chapter 7, the main impetus for an explosive silver demand that will not be able to be met by the available refined silver above ground will come from China. China, the USSR, the emerging countries of Africa, even the eventual (one hopes) peaceful growth of Middle Eastern nations – will all contribute to a future demand for silver by the year 2000 that will sap the available silver supply and strain new silver resources. Of course, unless one realises that the amount of silver used by a country is directly dependent on its population, it is difficult to foresee this coming explosive factor in the future silver price.

It takes time for silver to emerge in 999 purity from ore dug from the earth. It takes time to melt down silver in forks, knives and sterling spoons, let alone antique silver. And it is highly doubtful that when widespread silver demand explodes there will be enough refined silver to meet mankind's needs. That is primarily why I am utterly convinced that after China is electrified in a few years' time – so that its citizens can plug in the amenities of American life that use silver to provide entertainment and enjoyment – the resulting demand will sweep away upward price resistance.

Actually, the silver price today is quoted in dollars and in sterling, it is also quoted in the currencies of countries in free or managed economies. But I'm not intimating that the dollar will collapse against the strong currencies at some future date to such an extent that a $50 price will be the equivalent of a $5 silver price today. Nor am I saying that inflation such as Americans and Englishmen have never before experienced will cause silver to soar above $50 before the year 2000. At the risk of being both boring and repetitive I conclude that future silver demand coupled with future unavailability of supply to meet that demand will pressure the price past any silver owner's dreams.

In support of this theory, the peoples of the US, the UK, and on the free continent are capitalistically oriented. That is to say that when a material is used in industry it has to cost low enough for the fabricator or user to make a profit. In the case of silver, future explosive demand will come from the managed economy sectors where profit is not a primary consideration. So that if the Russians require silver above their own production, they assuredly will go into the market and buy it – without worrying about how much it costs in dollars. Similarly, the Chinese, who definitely will require far more silver by 2000 for their ever-growing population, will also enter the market.

Trading in silver from now until 2000, in my opinion, could be done effectively on a short-term, in-and-out basis. Some traders who go short silver in physical or paper form on strength and cover by buying on weakness may be able to make a lot of money, as well as lose it. Other traders who decide to seek trading profits in silver by going long on weakness and selling on strength may be able to make a lot of money, or lose it. But in my opinion silver *investors* who accumulate fully paid for metal and squirrel it away in safe depositories will win – even before 2000, especially if the private stockpile is accumulated under the going cost of American silver production.

In the meantime if the trading and accumulating lessons in this book turn out to be of assistance, then the work will have been genuinely worthwhile.

APPENDIX A

Sources for further information

1 Explanatory material anent silver leverage contracts, options on physical silver, and purchase of physical silver coins and bullion is available from MONEX International, 4910 Birch Street, Newport Beach, California. Phone: 714-752-1400.

2 Brokerage and bullion firms issue periodic silver reviews. Such firms are Goldman Sachs, Shearson Lehman Hutton, and Sharps-Pixley. For information about these reports apply directly to these firms which have addresses or agents in major cities of the world.

3 Handy & Harman, 850 Third Avenue, NYC 10022 publishes a complimentary annual silver review devoted to fundamentals of physical silver.

4 Bureau of Mines, Department of the Interior, Washington DC publishes a monthly *Gold & Silver* review. For information write to James O'Donnell, Bureau of Mines, 2401 E St, NW, Washington DC 20241.

5 The Silver Institute, 1026 Sixteenth St, NW, Washington DC, 20036 publishes a monthly silver information letter for $15 a year; and *New Silver Technology* (monthly at $275 per annum). For samples and full information about publications of this institute, write to John Lutley, Director at the above address.

6 *American Metal Market* is the only daily paper devoted exclusively to metals. For subscription information write to Ms Georgia Dusselot, *American Metal Market*, 7 East 12th Street, NY, NY 10003.

7 For background on silver fundamentals prior to 1980 read *Silver: The Restless Metal*, by Roy W. Jastram, Ronald Press div. John Wiley, NY, 1981. For the real story of the silver boom and bust 1979-80, read *Silver Bulls*, by Paul Sarnoff, Arlington House, (out of print) which may be in libraries or will someday be reprinted.

8 For the best in software anent silver futures and silver options on futures trading and evaluation, contact Jerry White, President, Software Options, COTS, 210 Sylvan Avenue, Englewood Cliffs, NJ 07632, or phone 201-568-6664.

APPENDIX B

Further reading

Chapter 1
National Geographic Magazine, September 1933 and September 1981.
Modern Silver Coinage, published by the Silver Institute, 1026 16th Street, Washington DC 20036, USA.

Chapter 2
Silver Refiners of the World and Their Identifying Marks, published by the Silver Institute, address as above.
Coin World (US).
Coin & Medal News (UK).
Australian Coin Review (Australia).

Chapter 3
Silver and Gold Report (Daniel Rosenthal, Editor/Publisher, 251 Lafayette Circle, Suite 310, Lafayette, California 94549, USA).

Chapter 7
New Silver Technology, published by the Silver Institute, address as above.
American Metal Market (Mike Botta, Editor-in-Chief, 7 East 12th Street, NY, NY 10003, USA).
Gold and Silver Monthly, published by the Bureau of Mines, Washington DC.
Metals Week (McGraw-Hill).
Engineering & Mining Monthly (McGraw-Hill).
Handy & Harman Silver Review.

Chapter 8
Jack Schwager, *A Complete Guide to the Futures Markets* (John Wiley and Sons, New York, 1984).

Chapter 9
Eugene Sherman, *Gold Investment Theory and Application* (New York Institute of Finance/Prentice Hall, 1986).
Jack Schwager, *A Complete Guide to the Commodity Markets*.
Robert Prechter, *Elliot Wave Theorist*.

GLOSSARY

ACCEPTABLE SILVER STOCKS: See *Certificated stocks, Exchange stocks.*

ACTIVE MONTH: A futures month which is actively traded, usually the month with the largest volume and open interest.

AGENT: An intermediary, who buys and sells for the client at the best available price, adding a commission to the purchase price and/or deducting a commission from the sales price.

AMERCIAN STYLE: This applies to the right of exercise of an option by the holder. Options exercisable in American style may be exercised on any trading day during the life of the option. See *European style.*

ANTIQUE SILVER: When the term 'antique' is applied to silver it is generally meant to identify nineteenth century and earlier silver. Antique American silver would range from the eighteenth century, whereas antique English silver, of course, would be of much earlier origin. Buyers of so-called 'silver antiques' would be well served to hire an appraiser before paying stratospheric sums for modern silver that may have been cast in ancient moulds or otherwise fraudulently 'antiqued'.

APPROVED DEALERS: These are wholesalers, who have been approved to deal directly with the United States Mint in the distribution of gold and silver coins produced by that mint. The wholesaler may also be a retailer.

APPROVED REFINER: A refiner whose output has been approved as acceptable for good delivery in fulfilment of physical silver market deliveries or futures exchange silver contracts. A list of approved refiners is available from involved exchanges and, for example, from Sharps-Pixley, of the London silver market.

APPROVED SMELTER: A smelter whose logo has been approved as acceptable for good delivery in fulfilment of physical silver market deliveries or futures exchange contracts. See *Approved refiner.*

ARBITRAGE: The arcane art of buying silver in one market and at the same time selling it for a profit in another. Or perhaps selling silver in one market and buying it for less in another. For example, go short CBOT silver (5 contracts of 1000 oz. silver) and simultaneously go long one 5000 oz. COMEX silver, etc.

ASSIGNMENT: The action of the clearing house in notifying an option writer the outstanding option has been exercised and the writer is automatically long or short the silver future as a result of the assignment. See *Option on futures.*

BACK MONTH: A silver future contract month that is far out. For example, in April 1988 a back month might be March of 1989, as opposed to the active (near month) May, 1988.

BACKWARDATION: An abnormal condition in the silver futures markets, where, because of tightness of available good-delivery silver, the near months trade at higher prices than the back months. See *Contango, Normal Market*.

BALL PARK FIGURE: A considered estimate, which, perhaps not precise, contains the ring of authority and approximates the real number. For example, the daily silver futures volume listed in the financial media, furnished by the exchanges each day. This figure, labelled 'estimate' would be a ball park figure.

BAR CHART: A chart constructed by technicians that reflects the high, low and closing price for selected sessions. An innovation of the familiar bar charts is the Japanese pole chart, which not only indicates the three major items of a bar chart but also reflects the opening price. See *Pole chart, Point & figure*.

BEAR SPREAD: A simultaneous long and short position in either silver futures or silver exchange traded options on futures which will generate limited profits with limited risk if the price of silver futures declines. The futures bear spread involves going long one month, then short another month. The options spread which can be accomplished with either exchange traded options on silver futures that are puts or calls involves the simultaneous purchase and sale of two silver puts or two silver calls with the same delivery month expiration. See *Contango, Option writing, Spread*.

BEARISH SPECULATOR: A misnamed 'investor' who is interested mainly in making money from a decline in the silver price.

BECKER PHENOMENON: Relying on the theory that the market is never wrong, Ulrich Becker, a successful commodity trader, will double up and enter the market the opposite way if his current long or short positions are stopped-out. See *Stopped-out*.

BREAKOUT: A technical term for a price movement that rises above the resistance limits of a trend line on a bar chart of silver price movements.

BREAKTHROUGH: The reverse of a breakout, the breakthrough is a down-side

violation of a trend line reflecting support levels on a bar chart of silver prices.

BULL SPREAD: This spread on either silver futures or options on silver futures is exactly the reverse of the strategies employed in the bear spread. It provides limit profits in the event of a silver price rise.

BULLION BANK: A bank that offers storage services to owners of bullion. It does not have to offer bullion loans, neither does it have to be a bullion dealer or bullion broker.

BULLION BROKER: An intermediary that arranges for purchase and delivery of physical silver on behalf of clients.

BULLION BUSINESS: The business of buying, selling, fabricating silver bullion to provide supply for industrial and investment silver markets.

BULLION COIN: A coin minted by governments to obtain something extra above the actual value of the silver inside the coin. In theory the bullion coin offers small investors the chance to accumulate silver in small quantities.

BULLION DEALER: This rubric covers bullion banks and bullion brokers who supply silver bullion in any form to the investment public. It also includes firms that actually deal in bullion, for instance, those who make up the silver fix each trading day in London and firms like Engelhard and Johnson Matthey who supply silver either in pure or alloyed form.

BULLION HEDGE: Holders of physical silver in storage or elsewhere, who are concerned about a silver price drop would go short silver futures as a hedge. Users of physical silver who might fear a future silver price rise could hedge by going long silver futures. Mining companies who would worry about a silver price drop could arrange a bullion hedge with a bullion dealer to assure a base price for silver to be mined at some future date. Investors who are concerned about possible future hyperinflation in the world could effect a bullion hedge by accumulating physical silver.

BULLISH SPECULATOR: A misnamed 'investor' interested in making money from a silver price rise.

BUTTERFLY: An exotic option strategy which involves the purchase of two silver options of differing strikes and the simultaneous sale of two silver options of the same strike. It also involves the purchase and sale of four of the same kinds of options (i.e. four calls or four puts). The butterfly can be vertical, horizontal, or diagonal.

BUY HEDGE: A user of silver who wanted to assure metal availability at a fixed price could make a buy hedge by going long silver futures of the contract month for which the price protection is desired. The user could also make a buy hedge with a bullion dealer in the physicals markets via options or leverage contracts.

BUY SIGNAL: An interpretation by a technically orientated speculator or professional that the pattern formed on his chart or charts indicates time to enter the market and buy. See *Sell signal*.

CALENDAR SPREAD: This is a spread in which the risk-taker buys an option on a silver future (put or call of a specific strike price) and simultaneously sells an option of the same strike for a differing month. See *Horizontal spread, Time spread*.

CALL: An option on silver physicals or futures for which the risk-taker pays a money premium for the right (privilege) to buy at an agreed contract price (strike price) a set amount of silver, in physical or futures form, at any time before an agreed expiration date (*American style*), or exercisable only on an agreed date (*European style*).

CASH & CARRY: A strategy where the holder of silver bullion sells it forward either in the physicals or the futures markets and the ensuing profit covers the cost of 'carrying' (storing) the metal.

CASH MONTH: See *Spot month*.

CASH SILVER: The prices listed in the financial press under the rubric 'Cash

Commodities' indicate: 1) the Handy & Harman price; 2) prices of other fabricators of the metal such as Engelhard; 3) the morning silver fixing in London, etc. In general, the cash price of silver is the Handy & Harman one, with adjustments. In the final analysis, the cash price of silver is made between buyers and sellers at the time of any actual transaction.

CERTIFICATED STOCKS (CERTIFIED STOCKS): Silver in standard bars, cast by approved refiners and smelters, and stored in approved exchange warehouses is considered 'certificated', because the silver has been inspected and has outstanding warehouse certificates reflecting the presence of the silver certified grade stored in an appropriate place. The exchange also reports on uncertificated stocks.

CFTC: These initials stand for Commodity Futures Trading Commission, an agency of the United States Government that came to life on 21 April 1975 and which registers financial intermediaries, such as commission merchants (including stockbrokers who trade futures), associated persons (brokers who service the public), and CTAs (commodity trading advisers) who manage money for clients. It is also the agency which investigates commodity frauds.

CHART PATTERNS: During the decades since Jesse Livermore, charts as bases for making trading decisions with futures have grown both in popularity and perhaps complexity. However, certain patterns revealing tops and bottoms of price trends are repetitive — especially since most traders tend to follow their formations.

CHARTING: The art of constructing graphs that can provide clues as to: when to enter and leave the market (long or short); where to place stop-loss orders; where resistance and support levels in a price trend occur, etc. See *Bar chart, Point & figure chart and Pole chart*.

CLEARING: When a trader effects a long-buy of a silver future in the pits of an exchange and another trader goes short that future, the process of notifying the person who actually bought and the one who actually sold, including the deposits of margin with the exchange clearing house, is termed 'clearing the trade.' Thus the account, who went long the future, receives a confirmation of the trade; the account, who went short, receives notice of the details of his risk; and the clearing member who acted for the buyer, and the one who acted for the seller, will each deposit the required exchange minimum margin with the exchange clearing house the following day.

CLEARING HOUSE: The corporation that guarantees the soundness and performance of trades occuring in the silver pits. Every trade (long and short) goes into the clearing house, so that the members responsible for the trade are identified, the margins collected, and changes in the equity of the open positions are adjusted (with money) on a daily basis.

CLEARING MEMBER: A member of the futures exchange who is also a member of the exchange clearing house. Financial requirements of clearing members are much higher and greater than those members of the exchange classified as 'non-clearing' members. Some clearing members trade only for themselves, others act solely for customers, others trade both for themselves and for the public, whilst some clearing members trade only for other members, etc.

CLOSE STOP: A stop-buy or stop-sell order that is within the range of the recent price fluctuations in silver. For example, if silver for a future month traded between $6.50 and $6.70 (a 20 cent swing) a close stop could be anywhere from ten to 20 cents higher or lower than the actual market.

COIN BAGS: These are bags of silver coins, $1,000 face value, of 90 per cent silver purity, and containing about 710 ounces of silver per bag. They used to contain $1,000 worth of silver dollars, half-dollars, quarters, or dimes minted before 1964. Because dollar bags have been used mainly to vend silver dollars individually to investors, the bag-buyer today gets circulated coins in bags of half-dollars, quarters or dimes, which are currently going in the market at a slight discount from the inherent value of the silver inside each bag. The New York Mercantile Exchange used to trade futures contracts of ten coin bags each, but ended such activity prior to 1980. Since then coin bags trade in a dealer market, such as made by MONEX.

COMEX: A registered futures exchange, whose members consist of commission merchants who: trade for themselves; trade for the public; and/or do both. Some trade only for other members. The nickname 'COMEX' stands for New York Commodity Exchange, which trades mainly gold, silver and copper futures, as well as options on those futures. For free exchange booklets anent any of the above items, write to: COMEX, 4 World Trade Center, NY, NY 10048, USA.

COMEX PRICE: The silver futures price last traded on the exchange. But during each trading session there is a spread in the price between the bid and the offer. Thus if May silver last traded at $6.75 on that exchange, the bid might be $6.80, the lowest offer might be $6.90, etc. See *Spot price*.

COMMERCIAL OPTIONS: These are generally long-term puts or calls on physical silver contracted between bullion dealers and industrial users and producers. See *Trade options*.

COMMISSION: A fee added to the price paid for a future or option purchase or deducted from proceeds of a sale, by the service firm. Some firms charge a half-commission when a futures position is entered; and then another half when the position is liquidated. Other firms charge no commission fee upon market entry, but charge a 'full' commission on market exit of that position. Commissions are also charged upon purchase and sale of options on futures. Since there are no fixed commissions, chances are the larger the trades the smaller percentage of the commission rates.

COMMISSION MERCHANT: A firm registered with the CFTC that is permitted to act as a broker for public clients in the purchase or sale on behalf of said clients in silver futures or silver options.

COMMODITY ACCOUNT: Speculators and hedgers, who use the services of registered commission merchants to buy or to sell silver futures or options on silver futures, have to open and maintain a commodity account at the service firm acting on their behalf, which means signing special account papers and forms permitting the shifting of funds from stockbrokerage or cash accounts at that same commission merchant.

CONFIRMATION: The paper sent by the commission merchant to its customer describing the trade made on the client's behalf. Since there are two types of action in the trading pits, it is sensible to check whether: the confirmation is properly a buy or a sell; the market entry or exit points complied with the order given and; the commission charged for the trade is correct. In a word, it pays to check each and every confirmation.

CONJECTURAL STOCKS: The appellation given to the estimates of silver bullion held by private investors.

CONSIGNED SILVER: Silver bars that may be on location at a silver user but actually belong to a bullion source. As the user removes the bars from their 'consignment' and melts them down, he pays the bullion source. Certain firms like Johnson Matthey will keep silver which has been sold to dealers in pooled storage, drawing from these stocks if the dealers demand delivery. This silver, which is pooled and not segregated by customer may also be called 'consigned silver'. See Pooled silver.

CONSUMPTION: A good deal of silver is lost each year in negatives that lie around the house, in x-ray pictures that have to be kept for records for many years in doctors' offices and hospitals. Unlike gold, which is virtually impervious to action of elements at normal temperature and pressure, silver does form compounds with other elements and a lot of silver is lost because the items turned black or dark brown and the owner did not realise a little polish could recreate its lustre. Silver in paints and graphics is not normally recycled; and dental and medical silver is rather dificult to be returned as salvageable scrap. So whilst most of the gold in jewellery, coins etc, is eventually recycled, a lot of silver is lost or 'consumed'. This annual figure, related to the apparent demand is an estimate called 'consumption'. See Demand.

CONTANGO: In a normal precious metal futures market, the going prices for further out futures months are higher than the prices for the nearby months. The annual difference between say December 1988 and December 1989 silver is mathematically equivalent to the rate charged for bond loans that have repossession clauses in them. Thus, as time passes, if the silver price remains stagnant in the cash market, the futures price would decline as the back months progressed towards the front of near months. Since the difference between the active and the back months is a mathematical number, spreads are popular with traders who believe the contango will widen or narrow. See Backwardation.

CONTINGENT ORDER: This is an order that becomes effective, if the market gets to a specified price and triggers a possible trade in this manner. The order may read, "If the May silver reaches $7.00 go short one July silver at market." Or, "If my May silver is sold at $7.00 buy the July at market." etc. Some brokers will not take any type of contingent order because they may not have either the personnel or the traders to actually watch markets that closely. At any rate for a contingent order to become a real order, something first has to happen to either an existing position or to a market price.

CONTRACT: All silver futures and options, whether in the physical markets or the paper markets are traded via contracts. Physical contracts are generally followed by actual delivery, receipt and payment of the metal, whilst futures and options on futures are mainly liquidated via offset without any physical silver being involved at all.

CONTRARIAN: A silver trader who believes the majority of the analysts letter writers, and assorted savants at brokerage firms, are wrong. If the consensus of opinion is that silver prices should rise, then the contrarian goes the other way. The contrarian goes not only against opinion, but also against the trend.

CONVERSION: In options terminology, conversion is the act of changing a position from a put to a call in a riskless fashion as follows: If a call is desired in a rising market, the strategist buys a put, goes long the silver future and sells a silver call. Theoretically in a rising market silver calls carry a larger premium than silver puts. So the converter buys the put, protects the acquired long position in the future with said put and sells a call on the protected future. His profit, of course, lies in the excess in the premium paid for the call by the buyer above the transaction costs of buying the put and going long the future by the converter. No matter which way the thereafter goes during the term of the options, the trader cannot lose any money. See *Reverse conversion*.

CORNER: When an individual or group has held long silver futures far in excess of available refined silver that fits exchange standards, and the individual or group holding the open long silver contracts demands delivery instead of liquidating the contracts by selling them, there is a possibility that the resulting squeeze on the shorts would be such that they would not be able to produce silver for delivery in time and the holders of the buy contracts (the longs) might have 'cornered' the market. It is, of course, illegal to effect a corner in silver or any other commodity traded under CFTC rules. See *Silver situation*.

COST OF CARRY: The theoretical cost of holding silver bullion from the present to the end of a future delivery month. A formula for this is to be found on page 66.

COVER: Although Webster's reflects many meanings for the word 'cover', when it comes to trading in silver, a short sale is "covered" (liquidated or offset) via a purchase of a similar future. When a risk-taker delivers cash to meet a margin call he has 'covered' the call. An option writer uses a long silver future to cover a short call and a short future to cover a short put.

CTA: This stands for Commodity Trading Adviser, a professional who is registered with the CFTC, manages money that is risked in futures markets for clients and charges a fee for said management. Before doing business with any CTA the risk-taker should ascertain what the charges are and what experience the CTA has had in applying his trading system.

DAY ORDER: An order to buy or to sell a silver future or option on a silver future that is for the day only, is aptly termed a day order. If the order is not executed in the pits during that day's trading session it automatically dies. See *GTC order*.

DAY TRADE: A futures or option on futures long or short position which is liquidated at a profit or a loss on or before the end of the session during which the position originated. See *Overnight trade*.

DEALER OPTIONS: These are puts and calls on physical silver bars which are issued by dealers who take the risk involved in writing (selling) the options either directly to the public or through authorised agents. The options, of course, can be sold only back to the dealer, and the exercise of the options is as good as the dealer's statement of guaranteed delivery. Unlike exchange traded options whose guarantee of performance is backed by a clearing house, dealer options in the United States can only be created and sold by sources approved by the CFTC.

DEFICIT: In futures trading, accounts are squared daily with the clearing house and between exchange members and their customers. Any sums outstanding after 24 hours which are due and payable are considered, under the umbrella word 'deficit'. A service person who works on a split of the commission basis does not get credit for any commissions created whilst the account being handled is in deficit. Since title does not pass for the underlying silver until it is due to be delivered and paid for, market erosion of the risk-taker's entry points creates calls for additional money to prevent any future deficit, if such erosion should continue. Therefore, an account is considered to be in deficit from the moment more money is required until that requirement has been satisfied. If an account is liquidated because the added margin has not been delivered to the broker and upon liquidation a negative balance results, then that account remains in deficit until the customer makes good the loss. The largest silver deficits in all futures trading history (about $1 billion) occurred during the liquidation of the Hunt Brothers positions. Yet the hundreds of millions of dollars in deficits due to the involved stockbrokers, who acted as commission merchants for the beleagured brothers were repaid in full.

DELIVERY MONTH: Futures markets in silver trade as far out as 18 months at a time. Since these markets are what is known as seller's options markets, the buyer of say a July 1988 may have to wait at the pleasure of the seller until the last trading day in July if he wants actual delivery of the physical silver underlying the futures contract. However, the seller can deliver the silver to the buyer on the first notice day, which is the last business day of June, the month preceding the delivery month. See *EFP*.

DELTA: An exotic theoretical yardstick that reflects a hedge ratio to an option writer (seller) who may be taking risks in selling covered and naked options on silver futures. The delta for silver calls is always positive and is never greater than one. The delta for puts is always negative and can never be lower than -1. Thus a call option with a delta of $+1$ would require the writer being long one future for each call to be written. A call with a delta of .5 would require one long future for each two calls written, etc. See *Gamma*.

DEMAND: The annual needs for silver that is used in photography, x-ray, medical and dental, electronic and electical, mirrors and other important industrial uses. Since silver is indeed a valued, but affordable, precious metal, it is demanded in bar and coin form by intelligent investors. These combined needs annually represent silver demand. However, just as new mine silver has continually been overstated by government, so has silver demand and usage been understated for decades. Silver demand has a direct linkage to population growth in countries that want the same amenities of life that exist in the United States and the United Kingdom: fast colour film, washing machines, VCRs, computers, solar cells, etc. – all items requiring silver in their manufacture. And since World War II the annual new silver supply has been in severe deficit to the growing silver demand, which has been met only by recycling silver scrap, coin meltdown, and drawdown or existing silver stocks. See *Consumption*.

DEPOSITORY: A bank vault or other secure place where physical silver is stored on behalf of customers.

DIAGONAL BUTTERFLY: See *Butterfly*.

DISCLOSURE STATEMENT: A form to be signed by a customer of a commission merchant in connection with purchase and/or sale of options on futures, including silver.

DISCOUNT: The money deducted from the

proceeds of a sell transaction in a silver future or silver option where the service firm has acted as a principal instead of as an agent.

DOLLAR AVERAGING: A method of silver accumulation involving regular purchases of fixed amounts of dollars. This creates more silver in the portfolio than if the same dollars has been expended over the same time period to buy silver at set mathematical levels.

DOs: This stands for 'delivery orders'. See *Silver certificates*.

DOJI LINE: A point on a Japanese pole chart that indicates the silver market opened and closed at about the same price level. See *Pole chart*.

DOUBLE: A combination silver option that offers a buyer the privilege of both a silver call and a silver put, except that if one side of the double (either the call side or the put side) is exercised, the other side dies.

EFP: These initials stand for 'exchange for physicals'. If a holder of a long silver future contract that has months to run decides he wants the actual silver now, then it is possible for an arrangement to be made with a member on the exchange floor to surrender the future position and substitute it with delivery of the actual metal.

ENTRY: The price at which a trade is triggered on behalf of an account. It is the entry price from which eventual profit, loss, and daily increase or decrease in equity in the account is calculated by the commission merchant service firm.

EQUITY: The value of a commodity trader's or speculator's positions. If the position value increases, the account can withdraw the increase in equity without payment of interest to the service firm. If the equity drops past a certain point the account is called on to deposit more cash. Changes in equity are calculated daily, according to change from market entry points. See *Entry, Excess, Position*.

EQUITY SHARES: Shares of stock in companies whose primary production involves the mining of mainly silver ore, or in fabricators and users whose main products depend on silver.

EUROPEAN STYLE: Describes the exercise feature of an option that grants the holder the right to exercise only on the last day of life of the option. Premiums for European style options are, of course, less than those levied for American style options, which can be exercised at any time from the day of purchase to the expiry date. See *American style*.

EXCESS: The increase in value of an account over and above the margin deposit required to maintain the position of the account. The excess can be withdrawn without paying any interest and used for any other purpose, including the addition of other futures and/or options. If the market becomes adverse to the account's positions he will be asked to replace the excess withdrawn previously in order to meet and maintain the account at required levels. See *Deficit, Equity, Pyramiding*.

EXCHANGE MEMBER: A futures commission merchant who is registered with the CFTC and is a member of an organised futures exchange. He can service public clients, other members, or trade for his own firm. See *Clearing house, Clearing member*.

EXCHANGE MINIMUM MARGIN: The monetary deposit a clearing member must deposit for: going long or short a silver futures contract; purchase or sale of an option on a silver future. See *House margin*.

EXCHANGE STOCKS: Silver bullion listed by the exchange and owned by members and customers of members reposing in approved exchange warehouses. Increases and decreases in exchange stocks could affect the silver price beneficially or adversely.

EXCHANGE TRADED OPTIONS: Options on silver futures or options on silver physicals which are listed for trading on an organised exchange. The clearing house of the exchange guarantees performance if the holders exercise. See *Dealer options*.

EXIT: The price at which an open and existing future or option position is liquidated. The difference in money between the price of entry and the price of exit of that position is equivalent to the profit or loss on the trade. See *Entry*.

EXPIRATION DATE: The day on which a specific option on a silver future or physical expires or dies. The holder of the silver option must exercise a valuable option on or before the expiration date. After that date, the option has no value.

EXPOSURE: See *Risk*.

FABRICATION CHARGE: A charge added to the going price of silver by a vendor to cover the cost of striking or casting silver bars.

FACE VALUE: The face value of a coin containing silver today may be entirely different from the actual value of the coin. For example, the face value of a silver dollar struck before 1964 may be $1. But the coin itself may contain $5 worth of silver, forgetting about its value as a collectible.

FAST MARKETS: When buy and sell transactions in the silver futures or options pits accelerate to a point of frenzy, markets become to say the least 'fast'.

FILL: When an order has been completed it has been 'filled'. The price it was executed at is the symbol of a good or a bad 'fill'.

FINE SILVER: On a coin or medallion the words 'fine silver' signify 999 purity.

FINENESS: The purity of the silver in any object containing the metal is rated from zero to 100 per cent. Thus a coin containing 70 per cent silver would have a fineness of 700, one containing 90 per cent silver, a fineness of 900, etc. 999 silver is 99.9 per cent pure silver.

FLATTEN OUT: See *Liquidation*.

FORWARD PURCHASE & SALES CONTRACTS: See *Leverage contracts*.

FORWARD SILVER: Silver presold to a specific delivery date. If the contract is an LME one, a forward sale is three months away. Silver 'forwards' can be arranged for longer periods.

FRONT MONTHS: The futures in silver that are the nearest trading months. See *Active month, Back month*.

FUTURES ACCOUNT: See *Commodity account*.

GAMMA: This theoretical exotic yardstick, used in assessing options on silver futures, measures the change in the delta of a silver option in relation to change in the price of the underlying silver future.

GAP: The space on a bar chart that remains empty because the price of silver has jumped sharply up or down from its previously charted trading level.

GO LONG: To buy silver physicals, silver futures, or silver options. Any profits thereafter depend on a rise in the silver price − except going long silver puts, which depend for profit on a price drop.

GO SHORT: The short sale of a silver future or option. Any profits thereafter depend on a silver price decline − except for going short naked silver puts, whereby profits will ensue if the silver price rises.

GOLD/SILVER RATIO: A market yardstick comparing how many ounces of silver it takes to buy one ounce of gold. To obtain the ratio, divide the second London gold fixing by the London silver fixing of that same morning. Because in the futures market on COMEX silver and gold trade actively in alternate months, traders who play the gold/silver ratio usually select the December futures, since both gold and silver trade actively on COMEX for that same month. A trader expecting a drop in the gold price and stability or upward improvement in the silver price would go long one COMEX December silver future and simultaneously go short one COMEX gold future. A trader expecting a silver price drop and stability or a rise in the gold price would go long a COMEX gold future and short a silver one. For a century before 1986 it took about 33 silver ounces to buy one gold ounce in the free markets of the world. At this writing it takes about 70 silver ounces to equal the value of one gold ounce.

GOOD DELIVERY: Every futures exchange trading silver, and every organised physical market requires certain standards of shape, form, weight and purity for silver that is to be delivered in fulfilment of sell contracts on that exchange or in that organised market. In general, standard bars identified with the logo of an acceptable refiner will be satisfactory for the good delivery of silver in most markets.

GOVERNMENT STOCKS: Silver on hand in the vaults of central banks, treasury departments, and stockpiles of governments are labelled 'government stocks'. After World War II, the government silver stocks in the USA amounted to in excess of 3 billion ounces. Currently there is slightly more than 100 million ounces left.

GTC ORDER: The initials stand for 'good till cancelled'. Inevitably, many service firms will not accept GTC orders, but will accept only day orders. In cases where a firm will accept GTC orders from a customer, the service person has to re-enter the order every day as a day order if it has not been executed. Variations of GTC are GTW (good the week) and GTM (good the month).

HAIRLINES: Lines extending from market highs and lows to the box reflecting opening and closing silver futures prices on a pole chart. See *Pole chart, Doji line*.

HANDY: The Handy & Harman silver price which is aired every business day around the globe at about noon, New York time. The handy is used by dealers and users of physical silver to set base prices for purchases and sales. But during COMEX trading hours, the physical markets are influenced by the spot silver price.

HEAP LEACHING: See *Hi-tech mining*.

HEDGER: A commercial silver user or producer who uses futures markets to shift price risk to speculators. See *House margin*.

HEDGES: There are basically two silver hedges; a buy-hedge and a sell-hedge. Since the word 'hedge' means, in the case of silver, simply 'price protection', a user would effect a buy-hedge in futures or physicals to guarantee a set price at some time in the future when the silver is needed, and; a producer would effect a sell-hedge in futures or physicals in order to guarantee a floor price for the silver waiting to be mined. A bullion dealer might so short against silver inventory as a hedge, lifting the hedge when the silver in inventory is sold to a customer.

HEDGING: Shifting price risk to a speculator is the *raison d'etre* of the futures markets. Such risk-shifting by users and producers of silver is called hedging.

HEDGING INSTRUMENTS: Silver futures and options on silver futures and/or physicals are typical hedging instruments.

HI-TECH MINING: A polite name for strip mining of areas containing low grade silver and/or gold ore. The ore is scooped from the surface by giant mechanised shovels, loaded into trucks, crushed, pelletised, and spread on giant piles called 'leach pads'. The ore is then subjected to baths of weak cyanide solution which leaches the precious metals out of the ore as the liquid seeps through the pad. The resulting 'pregnant' solution is subsequently treated and the precious metals won.

HOCKED SILVER: Pledged silver as collateral for a loan.

HORIZONTAL BUTTERFLY: See *Butterfly*.

HORIZONTAL SPREAD: See *Calendar spread*.

HOUSE: A firm servicing commodity account customers is called a 'house'. As such, the house can: charge its own house margins for speculators and hedgers; charge its own rates of commissions for transactions and; order undesirable accounts to leave the house or, in some cases, refuse to accept an account. Generally, the know-your-customer rule abides because in volatile markets, the house is always at risk on behalf of customers who may be required to deposit more margins or may suddenly go into deficit. The house sets commission rates and charges for trading customers it services. These rates may not only vary between houses, but also between customers inside a specific house.

HOUSE MARGIN: The good faith deposit required of a customer to be placed in the account at the service firm. The size of this margin invariably is larger than the margin required of a clearing member, the exchange minimum margin. For example, exchange minimums for a 5,000 oz. silver future long or short might be $2,000. But a house margin for a customer who is a speculator might be $4,000. House margins for hedgers are lower than for speculators.

IDLE CASH: Cash balance in an account with no futures position. A good service firm will shift idle cash to generate income for customers. For example at some firms idle cash in excess of $10,000 is put into T-bills. At other firms, a minimum of $20,000 is required. Excess in an account containing futures positions can also be put into T-bills if the excess amounts to more than the amount set by the service firm or 'house' for this purpose.

IMPLIED VOLATILITY: A yardstick used in setting the size of an option premium. The greater the implied volatility, the higher the option premium.

INITIAL MARGIN (ORIGINAL MARGIN): The initial good faith deposit required of a customer by a service firm, part or all of which is sent to the clearing house of the exchange to protect the soundness of the clearing house.

INVENTORY: The silver bars held in storage by a commercial user or bullion firm.

INVESTOR: This case of mistaken identity in silver futures or options markets is better labelled 'speculator'. The only silver investors are the accumulators, who have 'squirreled' away silver bars and coins and are holding them fully

paid for to either give to relatives or sell during the next silver boom.

JOB LOT: A lot of physical silver less than the normal 'round lot'. For example, normal round lots trading on the London Metal Exchange are 10,000 oz. each. A contract on 1,000 oz. would be a 'job lot'.

JUNK SILVER: Although the appellation indicates any kind of old silver junk or scrap, in practice the term junk silver mainly applies to circulated silver coins.

LEGAL TENDER: Coins that are struck by a government mint of silver, and have a face value far less than actual intrinsic value have become quite a popular activity amongst at least 70 countries. The government mint that strikes the coins calls them 'legal tender' but no owner of these coins will use them to pay bills at the level of legal tender placed by the mints on the coins.

LEVERAGE CONTRACT: Originally created to accommodate commercial firms, the silver leverage contract has been adapted by innovative intermediaries into a viable retail item under the aegis of the CFTC in the United States. A leverage contract in many ways is similar to a futures contract except: (a) it runs much longer in time than a future; (b) it requires a greater initial deposit of margin money; (c) it is issued by the intermediary to the customer without the financial soundness of a clearing house, and; (d) it cannot be resold to anybody but the issuer.

LIFTING A HEDGE: The process of removing price protection by liquidating the hedge position in futures or options.

LIMIT-DOWN: When silver exceeded the exchange specified limit of decline during a single trading session, trading in silver futures halted until the price moved off the limit-down level. For example, during the silver situation of January 1980, if the silver price dropped by $1, trading stopped on that day.

LIMIT ORDER: A popular type of order to

buy or to sell a silver future or option on a silver future at a specific price level. If the price in the trading pits reaches the limit it may or may not be filled.

LIMIT-UP: The converse of limit-down, limit-up is the market conditon where the price has risen above the daily permissable price movement level, creating a suspension of market activity until the price moves back down off the limit. For example, during the silver situation of 1979, if the silver price advanced by $1 over the close of the previous trading session, then all activity was suspended in the pits.

LIMITED RISK LEVERAGE: This ideal can only be achieved by buying a put or a call on silver physicals or futures. The option provides leverage whilst at the same time limits any possible loss to its cost.

LIMITED RISK POSITION: These are spreads in silver futures or in silver options that limit loss, although the loss cannot actually be predetermined in advance. Understandably, because loss is limited, profits are also limited.

LIQUIDATION: If long a silver future or option on a silver future, the position is liquidated by selling it. If short a silver future or option on a silver future, the position is liquidated by 'buying it in'. Accounts that do not deposit margin on demand are liquidated. A synonym for liquidation is to flatten-out the position or the commodity account.

LME: London Metal Exchange, a terminal market.

LME PAPER: Contracts issued by LME members.

LME SILVER: Silver bought and sold through the services of members of the LME during ring trading and after. A great deal of 10,000 ounces is normal, and any silver delivered against forward contracts that come due must be of the grade of fineness and form and weight acceptable to that terminal market.

LOCKED-IN: When a long position is protected by a short in another silver future month, the position is locked-in until the short is liquidated.

LONDON FIX: Three members of the five member fixing firms of the London Gold Market meet at the offices of Mocatta & Goldsmid, bullion brokers to the Queen, to set the silver fixing each business morning. The resulting price is called the London Silver Fix.

LONG CALLS: When a risk-taker has purchased call options on silver futures or on physical silver. See *Call.*

LONG POSITION: When the risk-taker: holds silver bullion in storage or silver long futures in a commodity account; is long calls on silver futures or physicals, or is long silver leverage contracts. To profit from any of these positions, the silver price must rise. A long position in silver puts requires a silver price decline for profits.

LONG PUTS: When the risk-taker owns put options on silver futures or silver physicals and to profit must enjoy a silver price drop.

LONGS: Synonym for silver bulls.

LOWER STOP: The reduction in the level of an existing stop-order. See *Stop-order.*

MAINTENANCE MARGIN: Once a commodity position has been executed by a service firm for a client, that position, which has already been buffered by initial margin, must be maintained at levels set by the house that is servicing the account. To do this, if the account is long and silver declines, more cash margin must be deposited with the broker. If the account is short silver futures and silver rises, the account must put up more cash. This maintenance margin is professionally called the 'variation margin'.

MANAGING A HEDGE: Protecting silver which is, of course, volatile in price. Hedging is costly, since it entails commissions, fees, and possibly the deposit of substantial capital. Hedging, as price insurance, is sensible when the silver price is felt to be in the process of rising or falling sharply. So some commercial firms at first may be fully hedged, then shift by lifting some of the hedges to become partly hedged and in markets of stagnancy, simply remain unhedged.

MANAGING THE POSITION: An active silver futures trader, or silver options on futures trader, having built a position, now must manage that position within the boundaries of a preset trading plan by making transactions which will not exceed the limits of that plan.

MANIPULATOR: A silver manipulator in the definition of existing US rules can only be a silver buyer who demands delivery and buys so much silver that way in the futures markets that the shorts, who have raised the price as supplies of exchange stocks contract, cannot find enough refined silver to make delivery during, or at the end, of the spot month. See *Corner.*

MARGIN: Initial margin is the good faith money deposit required by the *house* servicing the investor. This margin can be cash or treasury bills. After the position has been installed (put on) the customer's equity is monitored constantly. Any maintenance or variation margin, therefore, must be in cash. An experienced trader maintains at the broker an account called a segregated account in which T-bills are deposited, so that when additional margins are required bills are liquidated, and when the position generates excess equity more bills are purchased, etc.

MARGIN CALL: The formal demand for more money may take the form of a telex, a FAX, or a telegram. Chances are most margin calls that will be immediately answered are relayed first to the customer by phone. If the call is not met promptly by the account the account is flattened-out or liquidated.

MARK-DOWN: When dealing with a principal in the silver physical market the mark-down is the discount from the quoted bid of the buyer. See *Agent.*

MARK-TO-THE-MARKET: Although exchange requirements provide a set percentage of the entry value of a silver futures contract, it may be house policy to have the customer keep supplying cash as the market behaves adversely, even though said cash injections might be more than the exchange required percentage.

MARK-UP: When buying silver from a dealer or coin shop who acts as a principal, the customer is usually subjected to a dealer 'mark-up' above the market price of silver, in lieu of a commission. See *Agent, Principal.*

MARKET-AT-CLOSE: This type of buy or sell order will trade. But the price of the trade may not be the price quoted in the press, because silver futures and options on silver futures have an opening and a closing range. Therefore, the chances are the price the customer will receive will vary slightly from the 'settlement' price published the following day in the press. See *Settlement price.*

MARKET-AT-OPEN: A market order to buy or to sell silver futures or options on silver futures at the 'opening' will be executed. But on the exchanges there is an 'opening range' of prices. The price resulting on a market-at-open order will fall within that opening range, but might not be the price published as the opening price in the newspapers.

MARKET ENTRY: See *Entry.*

MARKET EXIT: See *Exit.*

MARKET-IF-TOUCHED: This type of contingent order becomes a market order if the price of the silver future or the premium on the desired option on silver future is reached. Unlike the limit order, the market-if-touched will trigger a trade when the specified price is reached. However, the report from the pits might be slightly different from the price desired. See *Limit order.*

MARKET ORDER: This type of order is executed virtually immediately in the silver futures pits or the options on silver futures pits. However, because there is always a spread between what is being bid for and what is being offered in the trading areas at the time the order reaches the floor, the resulting price may cause either dismay or glee, as the case may be. Still the market order is the only order that guarantees the customer a fill unless trading has been suspended previously.

MEDALLION: Mementos of silver struck to commemorate an occasion of historic importance, or to immortalise personalities. The medallions may be struck from any metals, but for this book we are concerned only with silver. For example, certain silver mining companies like Coeur d'Alene, Hecla and Sunshine have struck medallions of pure silver for various company milestones. Silver medallions can range from quarter ounce to five ounces and are a convenient way of accumulating silver in small sizes at reasonable prices.

MEDALS: In the past, military medals contained silver, gold, etc. in significant quantities. Since the end of World War II the major portion of medals has been cast or struck in alloys of baser metals.

MELTDOWN: During World War II there was a shortage of copper. Since silver is one of the best electrical conductors the government melted down a massive amount of silver coins (circulated and otherwise) in order to provide the 900 million silver ounces required. There still exists a substantial supply of circulated silver coins in bags and otherwise which could make up part of the secondary supply of silver if demand dictated further meltdown.

MORGAN DOLLARS: Most popular silver numismatic American silver dollar collectible coin. See *Numismatics*.

MOVING AVERAGE: A ploy plotted on a bar chart, usually in differing colour ink, reflecting the progress of the silver price over weeks, for example, compared with the course of day-to-day action in the pits. When the path of the moving average crosses above or below the path of the daily silver price a buy or sell signal may be generated.

MUSEUM GRADE COINS: Perfect specimens. See *Rare coins, Numismatics*.

NAKED: Taking an option-writing risk without coverage of silver, silver futures, or options on silver. A synonym for *Uncovered*.

NEAR MONTH: See *Active month*.

NEW MINED SILVER: Silver produced annually by mining companies.

NEW POSITION: A newly acquired silver physical, future or option position that has not been in the account previously.

NEW SCRAP: Silver shavings and leavings from industrial operations.

NORMAL MARKET: See *Contango, Backwardation*.

NUMISMATICS: The arcane art of coin collecting and appraising. Since this activity is still unregulated by the US government it naturally follows that there is the opportunity for chicanery if not fraud. To prevent being bilked in the purchase of silver coins graded too high for the prices demanded, seek the services of an ethical appraiser. Rare coins may be purchased at auctions, and resold via the same outlets, however the value of the silver coins could vary widely from the grade they allegedly deserve.

OFFSET:The liquidation of a long position via sale of a similar future or option results in wiping out that position from the account and generating cash which would include the initial margin plus any profits on the trade or minus any losses. The liquidation of a short position via purchase of a similar silver future or option on a silver future results in eliminating that position from the trader's account and the concomitant generaton of cash which would include the initial margin for the position plus any profit or less any loss on the offset short. When a position is offset a purchase and sale (P&S) confirmation is generated. This confirmation divulges details of the P&S involved in the offset. See *P&S*.

OLD SCRAP: Silver scrap from recycled items containing silver, such as candlesticks, etc.

OLD SILVER SPREAD: It has been held that it takes at least five years for buyers of old silver objects, including old coins containing silver, to overcome the spread between what the buyer pays and what he could get upon resale.

OPEN INTEREST: This figure published from information divulged by the exchanges represents combined positions long and short that remain open and have not been liquidated via offset. For example, an account at one firm goes long a May silver future and an account at another firm goes short the same future. The buyer's trade and the short-seller's trade, if they are not liquidated during the session created, are combined to make a *single* open interest addition. If that open interest remains for a day or two and both the long and the short liquidate, a single open interest is deducted from the aggregate. To see how changes in open interest are employed by traders turn to page 95.

OPTION: See *Call, Put, Option on futures.*

OPTION BUYER: A sensible speculator, who seeks profits in rising and/or falling silver markets with limited risk, by purchasing silver puts and calls. The option buyer can never lose more than the involved option premiums if wrong. See *Options on futures.*

OPTION WRITER: A speculator, professional or otherwise, who hungers to earn part or all of the money premium paid by option buyers.

OPTIONS ON FUTURES: Purchase of a silver call option on a COMEX future gives the buyer for premium paid the right or privilege to acquire a long silver future at the agreed strike (contract) price at any time up to expiration of the option. Purchase of a put on a COMEX silver future gives the buyer for premium paid the right to deliver to the writer's (seller of the option) a long silver future at the strike price till expiration. The writing of a silver call option on a COMEX future generates an automatic short futures obligation in the writer's account: Writing a COMEX silver put creates an obligation similar to being long a future. If the holder of a COMEX

silver call exercises his call, an automatic long future position is delivered to his account by the clearing house via 'assignment'. If a holder of a COMEX silver put exercises that option, a long future is generated in the writer's account automatically by clearing house assignment.

OPTIONS ON PHYSICALS: Options on silver physicals are traded on some exchanges. But the major activity in options on silver physicals occurs with dealer options generated by firms like LME members: MONEX, MOCATTA and MULTIVEST. See *Dealer options, Trade options.*

OPTION PREMIUM: See *Premium.*

OPTION WRITING: Synonymous with options selling. This activity can be covered (a long future covers a short call: a short furture covers a short put), uncovered, or partly covered. The writer of a naked call on silver deposits initial margin as if for a short silver future (plus the premium received). The writer of a naked put deposits initial margin as if long a silver future (plus the premium received). Thereafter, if the open position in the outstanding option deteriorates against the writer, more cash must be added to the account. If the premium on the open option declines, the writer can use the amount of the decline because it is an increase in his equity.

ORIGINAL MARGIN: See *Initial margin.*

OVERNIGHT TRADE: A silver long or short future or option position that is not liquidated during the day of its initiation but remains 'open' in a member's account or in the account of a customer of an exchange member. Usually the house commission rates for overnight trades are higher than for trades in-and-out of the market in a single trading session. See *Day trade.*

P&S: This stands for 'purchase and sale'. And whenever an existing long or short silver future or long or short option on a silver future is liquidated, a confirmation showing this activity is generated by the service firm and sent to the customer. If the account has more than one position, the P&S should be scrutinised to see that the proper position has been liquidated and the proper funds recouped, etc.

PAPER SILVER: Contracts traded in the world of paper silver, such as on exchanges like COMEX, Chicago Board of Trade, *et al.* are rarely combined with eventual performance. About 98 per cent of all silver futures traded anywhere in the world are liquidated via offset at profit or loss rather than accompanied by delivery, acceptance and payment for the underlying metal. Since the majority of options on silver that are traded can also be resold into the pits on or before expiration, if they have value, the creation of options on silver futures merely adds to activity in the futures if the options are successful. Thus, the claim that a futures exchange is the world's largest metal exchange should not be taken seriously: COMEX, of course, is the world's largest paper silver exchange.

PHYSICAL SILVER: Usually found in standard bars of approximately 1,000 oz. (70lbs), for industrial and serious trading purposes, the world of physical silver also includes smaller bars, bullion and legal tender silver coins. Purity can vary: with pure silver considered 99.9 per cent pure; sterling, 92.5 per cent pure; coin silver, mainly 90 per cent pure, etc. The bulk of the retail trade in physical silver has been conducted in coin shops. But in recent years New York Stock Exchange members have entered into that activity, including Merrill Lynch, Paine Webber, Prudential Bache, Dean Witter, etc. Since many states levy sales and use taxes, intelligent investors accumulate and store their silver in banks in the state of Delaware and the State of Rhode Island where such an onerous levy does not exist. On the Continent there are areas where a value added tax is levied on silver purchases, which is perhaps why during the past decade Zurich has greatly enlarged its silver storage vaults.

POINT & FIGURE: A system of charting which involves financial tic-tac-toe (generally x's and o's) to depict trend reversals. Time passage and volume are omitted items, but are generally plotted on bar charts.

POLE CHART: Created by a Japanese genius this type of chart proves quite effective in forecasting short-term silver price movements. The chart reflects not only the open and closing prices during a trading session, but also the high and low prices for that said session. The area between the daily high and low is filled in solidly with ink: an up-day is red; a down-day is black. And the high and the low prices are connected to the box connecting the open and close. These lines leading to the opening price and to the closing price are called 'hairlines' and they are significant to the analysis of the chart. The patterns formed by the lines and the filled-in boxes of the pole chart indicate strength, weakness, and reversals or turning points. Further information about pole charts can be obtained from the following authoritative source: Market Strategies, 7666 Caffey Lane, San Diego, California 92126, USA: Telephone (619) 578-0733.

POSITION: The inventory of silver in physical form would be the physical position of a silver trader. Long and short silver futures would be the futures position. Long or short silver options would be the options position. And the condition of a trader's account would reflect the cash position. A silver trader does not always know what the market might do tomorrow, but he should always know what his position is today.

PREMIUM: The money fee paid by a buyer to the writer of a silver option. Components included in the premium are: a) time to expiration; b) volatility and; c) strike price related to price in the market of silver physical or future underlying the option.

PRINCIPAL: In the silver milieu, a bullion source that buys silver in refined and concentrate form and sells fine silver for a net price as opposed to an agent who buys and sells silver at net prices plus or minus a commission.

PRODUCTION: The monthly, quarterly and annual fundamentals reflecting new mined silver. The record indicates that estimates of annual production published each year by the United States Bureau of Mines have been grossly overstated. This has helped keep the silver price depressed because it adds to the silver availability.

PROMOTION: The most promoted precious metal in the world is gold: the least promoted precious metal is silver. For more than 40 years a continuous campaign of negative promotion designed to divorce the word precious from silver and to relegate it to an industrial metal like the base metal copper has been successfully waged by an association of silver users. It was not until 1987 that the silver producers in the United States formed a promotional body called Silver International to develop educational and marketing programmes that will increase consumer understanding, interest and desire for a variety of silver merchandise, including investment products. Should the promotion launched in 1987-88 by the six leading silver mining companies in North America also be supported by the silver mining giants in Mexico and Peru, promotional funds will be available to correct public misconceptions that silver is not precious.

PROMPT DATE: Silver trades in the LME ring via 10,000 oz. contracts issued by LME members. Each contract specifies the term of the trade and sets a date when the actual delivery of the LME warehouse receipt (warrant) covering the involved silver bars must be presented to the buyer and payment rendered to the seller. This date (next day for cash silver and 90 days for forward silver) is called the 'prompt date', which never falls on a Saturday, Sunday or a British Bank Holiday

Monday. From then on, LME silver contracts are created until they are settled. The buyer can resell the contract but only for the prompt date on the contract. Thus in Mid-April a buyer of 10,000 ounce 3-month LME silver might receive a contract with a prompt of Thursday, 14th July. Unlike transactions on COMEX no specific initial margin must be deposited during the term of the contract, but margin and maintenance margin might be requested by the house involved.

PUBLIC OUTCRY: Most of the transactions in the silver pits are done between buyer and seller via open outcry and finger-waving to indicate how many lots the shouters are buying and/or selling. Certain trades like EFPs and silver spreads are exceptions. EFPs are ex-pit transactions, while silver spreads are arranged for a mathematical difference between the involved trading months and the actual level of buying and selling of the involved futures are set by a 'spread-maker'.

PUT: The opposite of a call. The buyer of a put pays a money premium to the writer of the put for which the buyer retains the privilege of selling to the writer a specified lot of physical silver or a silver future if the put is an option on a future at the agreed strike at any time to expiration. In effect, the purchaser of a put is similar to a short-seller of silver, but without the upside risk. Some investors or commercial firms that have physical silver on hand or in inventory may resort to purchase of puts for protection.

PYRAMIDING: Adding to existing long or short silver futures positions as the market price direction turns favourable.

RAISE STOP: A trader in silver futures may be long or short of said futures and options on silver futures. As part of his trading plan he may raise existing stop order levels. See *Stop orders*.

RARE COINS: The coins that bring big prices at coin auctions, not the ones classified in advertisements revealing discovery of a rare find in hardly circulated coins, etc. See *Museum grade coins.*

RECYCLED SILVER: Silver that is added to existing supply through refinement of scrap and coin meltdown is recycled.

REFINED SILVER STOCKS: Apparent levels of silver in refined form at reporting smelters and refiners.

REFINER: A bullion source that takes concentrated ore, scrap, silver for recycling, melts them down and refines the metal into several states of purity. The refiner can also create alloys of silver with other metals to meet the needs of customers. And at times innovative refiners also act as bullion dealers in helping customers hedge their silver needs for the future.

REPO RATE: This is the rate which a financial intermediary charges a customer for a secured loan that contains a repurchase agreement. This rate is approximately the same as the difference between the silver futures trading months. See *Contango.*

RESISTANCE: An assumed ceiling along a rising trendline. See *Breakout.*

REVERSALS: Points on a chart that herald changes in the trend.

REVERSE CONVERSION: In this riskless trading strategy, a silver call on the future is bought, the future underlying the call is sold short, and a covered put on that future is written and sold. See *Conversion.*

REWARD: See *Risk/Reward Ratio.*

RING DEALING: Silver trades on the LME morning and afternoon inside a ring formed by representatives of ring-dealing LME members. Trade in silver, and other LME metals, conducted during the morning and afternoon 'rings' are considered ring dealings.

RISK/REWARD RATIO: Every entry into any of the silver markets entails capital risk. Profits upon successful exit generate monetary rewards. In the paper world of silver futures and options a trader should not take the risk unless the contemplated trade is considered to have the chance of returning three times the risk as a reward, that is a risk/reward ratio of 3-to-1.

RISK: See *Risk/Reward Ratio.*

SALES & USE TAX: Many states in the USA, with notable exceptions of Delaware and Rhode Island, do not levy a sales and use tax on silver purchases. To avoid this tax, no matter what state in which the investor resides, all he has to do is buy silver in any state and never take delivery. For example, if a New York resident buys silver in Delaware, he does not pay tax. But, if he drives to Delaware, picks up the silver from a bank, and takes it back to New York, he is liable for the sales and use tax which is 8 per cent plus at this writing.

SELL SIGNAL: Depending on what chart system a trader uses, he probably will use formations that signal a sale to either liquidate long positions or install shorts.

SEMI-NUMISMATIC COINS: Silver legal tender coins like the proof Walking Liberty $1 silver coin may have eventual numismatic value. Since they command a premium over the brilliant uncirculated legal tender silver dollars minted in 1986 and 1987, the silver proof coins of those years are semi-numismatic. So are the Japanese silver Hirohito coins and the Chinese silver panda coins.

SERVICE FIRM: See *House.*

SHEKEL: An ancient Hebrew silver weight of 252 grains. Currently, the silver shekel is the official money of Israel.

SHORT CALLS: A condition in an option writer's account who has written call options on silver futures or physicals. See *Option writing.*

SHORT POSITION: In silver parlance, the trader is bearish and aims to replace the short futures in silver by buying them in at a lower level. If the short position involves naked or uncovered calls, to cover when the call premiums dwindle down because of time erosion or because of a decline in the silver price.

SHORT PUTS: A bullish ploy in an option

writer's account where puts are sold short without going short the future in stable or rising silver markets. See *Option writing*.

SHORTS: Silver bears.

SILVER BULLION: See *Physical silver*.

SILVER BULLS: See *Silver investors*.

SILVER CERTIFICATES: In 1987 a Mexican bank issued certificates for sale to citizens reflecting small amounts of silver actually stored at the bank. The certificate holder or purchaser could either take delivery at some future date of the amount of silver underlying the certificate, or simply resell the certificate for value.

SILVER CONSUMPTION: See *Consumption*.

SILVER FLATWARE: Table silver fabricated from Sterling silver, which is 92.5 per cent pure silver and 7.5 per cent copper. Much of the business formerly involving the manufacture of silver forks, knives, spoons etc. has been lost to similar utensils fabricated from stainless steel.

SILVER FUNDAMENTALS: These are the numbers that analysts use to monitor activities in the supply/demand silver equation.

SILVER INVESTORS: Bullish individuals who accumulate and hoard physical silver, without ever selling.

SILVER LEASING: During periods when refined silver is in short supply or 'tight', traders have been known to borrow silver bars for delivery, hoping to replace the bars when the price of silver drops. In another application, bullion firms may lease silver to customers for inventory purposes, with the clients paying for the silver if they consume it. See *Consignment*.

SILVER OPTIONS: These are: puts and calls and doubles on LME silver; puts and calls on physical dealer options and; puts and calls on exchange traded silver futures. See *Option writing*.

SILVER SHARES: See *Equity shares*.

SILVER SITUATION: The boom and bust, so-called 'manipulation' of 1979-80. See *Silver bulls* by Paul Sarnoff, Arlington

House, 1980; and *Beyond Greed*, Viking, 1984.

SILVER SULFIDE: Normally 999 silver does not tarnish. But sterling silver, which contains 92.5 per cent pure silver and 7.5 per cent copper, may react when exposed to air containing sulfurous fumes to form silver sulfide, a dark brown tarnish. A little polish and rubbing with a soft cloth on this tarnish brings out sterling's true lustre.

SILVER SURPLUS: The above-ground silver supply that the users consider as available if new production declines and which, of course, exceeds by far the annual needs of industrial firms worldwide.

SILVER SWAPS: As with gold, silver in New York can be readily swapped (exchanged) for silver in London. Exchange of COMEX warehouse receipts, for example, for LME silver warrants would be a silver 'location' swap. Another form of swap may occur between a user who has standard bars in inventory but requires an alloy of silver for fabrication needs. The user exchanges the standard bars for the alloy by payment of a modest fee.

SILVER TECHNICALS: Formations on charts that reflect changes in price, volume, open interest, patterns etc. which are interpreted as bullish or bearish by technically orientated traders.

SILVER TRADE DOLLAR: In the days when silver was the real part of money, coins were struck to be used in transactions with many provinces, municipalities and areas of the Far East (China, in particular). Since 1979, however, there have been so many fraudulent 'trade-dollars' stamped out of brass and silver coated, the best advice is simply to avoid these.

SUA: These initials stand for Silver Users Association, founded in 1947, whose altruistic aims include achieving low silver prices in the industrial market places of the world for its members.

SMALL BARS: Silver bars less than 1,000 oz. each. Popular sizes range from cast or struck 100 oz. bars down to one ounce stamped silver ingots.

SPECULATOR: While this term may sound nasty in share dealings, the speculator is an essential ingredient of the futures market. He or she is the bullish or bearish risk-taker to whom hedgers (silver users and producers) shift their price risks. Without the speculator there would be: no viable silver futures markets and; no price volatility.

SPOT MARKET: The price of silver quoted to buyers or sellers of cash silver for immediate delivery (24 hours) is called the spot market silver price. See *Handy, London Fix*.

SPOT MONTH: Futures trade on exchanges, understandably, in contracts calling for silver purchase and/or sale during specified 'future' months. But as the far out months are gradually moved towards the present, these future months become eventually the current or calendar month of the present. This current month is termed the 'spot month'. The spot month, which is of course the delivery month, is also called the 'cash month' on silver future exchanges.

SPOT PRICE: See *Spot silver*.

SPOT SILVER: The price for cash silver, or spot silver, is eventually made by the person most anxious to do the business. During trading hours on COMEX the price dealers quote is not taken from the COMEX spot month, but rather adjusted from the last trade in a COMEX active month.

SPREAD: The purchase of a silver future and simultaneous short sale of a differing month future is called a 'spread'. Futures spread in silver narrow or widen according to interest rates and underlying price of the metal. A spread of options on silver futures involves the simultaneous purchase and sale of put or call options in any of the following manner: 1) buy call expiring in a delivery month at a specific strike price and simultaneously sell a silver call at the same strike for a differing delivery month; 2) buy put expiring in

one delivery month at a set strike and simultaneously sell put at the same strike price for a differing delivery month; 3) buy call for a set delivery month at a specific strike price and simultaneously sell a call for that same delivery month with a differing (higher or lower strike); 4) buy put for a delivery month at a specific strike price and simultaneously write a put for the same delivery month at a differing strike. The strategies in numbers 1 and 2 above result in horizontal silver options spreads, creating a debit or credit to the option writer's account. Strategies in numbers 3 and 4 are called vertical options spreads and also result in a debit or credit to the writer's account. Spread in a silver future quote from the floor indicates the bid and the offer; the same with a quote on an option on a silver future. And spread in the physical silver world stands for the difference between where the silver source can do business (his cost) and the price the silver is proffered to the customer.

SPREAD-MAKER: A popular term for a floor trader who specialises in making markets in spreads on silver futures.

SPREAD ORDERS: In effecting silver futures spreads, orders are entered reflecting the difference which the potential customer desires to enter the market. Assuming the difference in March 1988 between the May and July silver futures is 9 cents an ounce and also that a risk-taker believes this will narrow to 7 cents before May becomes the spot month; and, finally, that the potential spreader wants to therefore go short the July silver and long the May contract at 9 cents, the spread order would read 'buy May COMEX silver and sell July COMEX silver – with a premium of 9 cents an oz. July over May'.

SQUEEZE: See *Corner*.

STANDARD BAR: About the size of a one pound loaf of bread, but narrower on the top than on the bottom a standard silver bar weighs approximately 1000 troy ounces. It bears the hallmark (logo) of the source that cast the bars and generally the storage source has appended a paper sticker or tag providing precisely the exact weight (999 oz. or 1001.5 oz), purity and source (smelter/refiner), plus the number of the warehouse receipt or warrant which signifies that specific bar is in storage at the warehouse issuing the receipt or warrant.

STATEMENT: A monthly summary of activity and condition in the account of a customer who trades in futures and options on futures. This *must* be carefully checked against confirmations received during the month covered by the statement for errors, etc. The statement, in sum, describes each and every transaction, lists all the long and short open positions in silver futures, options on silver futures and physicals in the position of the account at the service firm.

STERLING SILVER: 92.5 per cent silver: 7.5 per cent copper. See *Flatware*.

STOP ORDER: This is a protective device used by traders to limit losses in long or short futures and options on silver futures positions. If the market reaches the stop point the order is triggered. As a result, using stop buy and stop sell orders could result in poorer executions than if the traders had simply exited at the market. The price on a buy-stop order is always *higher* than the existing market; and the price on a sell-stop order is always *below* the market. It is the popular opinion in the pits that 'Trading with stop orders is like playing the market with marked cards . . .'

STOPPED OUT: A condition that exists when a stop order is executed and the trader is left without his position and the adverse market suddenly turns favourable. This results in the trader being 'out' of the market.

STRADDLE: In futures this is similar to the word 'spread'. In options on silver futures a risk-taker could buy both a silver put and a silver call, say for the same expiration month and at the same strike price, and consider he has purchased an option 'straddle' because profits could ensue, no matter which

way the market goes during the life of the straddle – if the premiums received on liquidation exceed the cost of purchasing the straddle. A straddle whose strikes are away from the market (the strike of the call is above the market: that of the put, below the market) is called a 'strangle'.

STRANGLE: See *Straddle*.

STRENGTH: Market condition when the silver price is rising and sufficient bullish speculators are present to absorb the normal hedging (short-selling) trades of professionals.

STRIKE PRICE: The contract price of a silver option on physicals or futures. This can be 'at market', 'in-the-money' (below market for call: above market for put), or, 'out of the money' (above market for call: below market for put), where the strike price of an option impinges on its daily premium.

STRUCTURING A HEDGE: Since a hedge is costly and has to be tailored to fit the needs of a potential commercial user or producer it has to be structured (a fancy term for 'planned'). Key elements to be considered in this connection are: 1) how much silver has to be involved in the hedge; 2) how long does the hedge have to run; 3) what hedging devices are to be employed and; 4) how much the exercise will cost. Once a hedge has been properly structured it must be installed (put on) – thereafter, it must be managed. For assistance, contact the author via the publisher.

SUPPLY/DEMAND: If the available supply of silver is less than the demand from industry and investors, the price rises. If the available supply of silver is greater than the demand by industry and investors the silver price expectedly drops. Handy & Harman's annual *Silver Review* is the most popularly watched summation of silver demand and supply.

SUPPORT: A theoretical floor price area delineated by trend lines on bar charts. Theoretically if the silver price breaks down below the support line it could go lower. See *Resistance*.

TECHNICAL MARKET: A commodity market where physicals are bought and sold to settle contracts made by members of that market rather than to settle those contracts by liquidation via offset: See *LME*.

TIGHTNESS: A condition in the silver physical market where there is not enough refined silver readily available to meet delivery demands.

TIME SPREAD: Synonymous with *Calendar spread*.

TRADE: This simple word has many meanings: 1) the purchase or sale of a lot of physical silver is a trade; 2) the purchase or sale of a silver future is a trade; 3) the purchase or sale of an option on silver physicals or silver futures is a trade; 4) members of commodity exchanges who are involved in some facet of commercial aspects of silver are dubbed with the nickname 'the trade'; 5) every entry into the silver physicals, futures, or options on physicals or futures is termed a trade, etc.

TRADE OPTIONS: These are silver options to buy or to sell physical metal made between bullion sources and commercial users and producers. They are outside of the regulatory scope of the CFTC and other agencies.

TRADER: A person who buys and sells physical silver, futures, or options on futures or physicals as a means of making a living.

TRADING ON THE EQUITY: If positions in silver futures create excess cash because of favourable price direction, and the trader adds to the existing position with funds created by an increase in his equity, he has been 'trading on the equity'.

TRADING PLAN: Every silver trader should preconstruct a sensible plan before trading begins.

TRADING SESSION: On the LME, silver trades twice in the morning rings and twice in the afternoon rings in five minute sessions. On COMEX silver trades from 9 a.m. to 2.30 p.m. NY time. A single day's activity is called a 'session'.

TRAILING STOP: A stop loss order that is regularly raised as the price of silver advances, or regularly lowered in instances of silver price declines. In effect, this practice 'trails' the trend of the market.

TRANSACTION FEE: A charge levied upon a customer for having a service firm execute trades on the customer's behalf. The fee could include commission, floor brokerage fees, and CFTC fees. Since there are no fixed commissions, customers who are quite active find they can be benefited by lower rates and fees upon demand, whilst those who seldom trade may find fees proportionately higher than those levied on active traders. See *Commission*.

TREND: The path of the silver prices in physical and paper markets over a period of time may form a rising or declining trend, or may be trendless. Often technical traders consider both the major trend in the price path and the minor trend. In a trendless market money is made simply by going short silver futures in a back month and liquidating (covering) the short by buying and offset to profit from the contango.

TREND LINES: Solid lines connecting tops and bottoms of silver prices on bar charts. Some technicians also connect the closing prices. The trend lines indicate ceilings of support and resistance.

TREND-FOLLOWING SYSTEM: Trading silver futures and/or options on futures, technicians mainly follow the trend without trying to get into the market at the bottom of a trend or getting out at the top of a trend, but rather to enter the market when a trend becomes evident and exit it before the trend reverses.

UNCOVERED: See *Naked*.

UNCERTIFICATED STOCKS (UNCERTIFIED STOCKS): Stocks of silver that do not have warehouse certificates in circulation.

VAT (VALUE ADDED TAX): An onerous

burden on investors designed to enrich governments that levy such a tax. See *Sales & use tax.*

VERTICAL BUTTERFLY: See *Butterfly.*

VERTICAL SPREAD: See *Spread.*

VOLATILITY: A measure of the degree of silver price change from price in the previous session. As applied to options on silver futures, the degree of reaction in premium costs to changes in the preceding options session. Volatility in silver options (physical and on futures) is part of the makeup in the premium and the delta of an option.

VOLUME: Each day the volume of trading on silver futures exchanges is published for the press and members. But this 'volume' is a 'ball park' number. The real volume is published the following day (two days after the trading session).

WAREHOUSE RECEIPTS: Certificates describing bars of silver stored in exchange approved warehouses which are negotiable and issued to a bearer. These certificates are transferable and are used: 1) as collateral for loans on the physical silver covered by the certificates or; 2) presented by a short seller as good

delivery in the liquidation by that method of his obligation to deliver metal. See *Warrants.*

WARRANTS: These are certificates representing ownership of silver stored in approved LME warehouses. See *Warehouse receipts.*

WEAKNESS: Absence of speculators of a bullish nature creates trading sessions or parts of sessions dominated by professional short sellers of silver futures and silver options. See *Strength.*

WEIGHT: With respect to physical silver, the troy system of weights is used, just as in the case of the other precious metals such as the gold and the platinum group.

WHIPSAW: A trader's condition when he has been naked a strangle and is hit by exercise on both sides because of a violent up and down market.

WHOLESALE PRICE: Generally, the silver price considered 'wholesale' is the Handy. See *Handy.*

WRITER: A seller of options on silver futures or physicals.

WRITING: The arcane art of making money by the legal bookmaking exercise called 'option writing'. See *Option writing.*

INDEX